Honky Tonk

There'll always be a honky tonk
With a jukebox in the corner
And someone crying in their beer
And one old hanger-oner
Someone looking lonely
From a losin' love affair
Yes, there'll always be a honky tonk somewhere

"There'll Always be a Honky Tonk Somewhere,"
BY JOHNNY MACRAE AND STEVE CLARK

HonkyTonk

Portraits of Country Music 1972–1981

BY **Henry Horenstein**

FOREWORD BY EDDIE STUBBS
AFTERWORD BY CHARLES MCGOVERN

CHRONICLE BOOKS

SAN FRANCISCO

For Ol' Sinc, Brian Sinclair
"Faster horses, older whiskey . . ."

Library of Congress Cataloging-in-Publication Data available.

ISBN 0-8118-3627-4

Manufactured in China.

Designed by Brett MacFadden

Distributed in Canada by Raincoast Books
9050 Shaughnessy Street
Vancouver, British Columbia V6P 6E5

10 9 8 7 6 5 4 3 2 1

Chronicle Books LLC
85 Second Street
San Francisco, California 94105

www.chroniclebooks.com

Page 2:
Interior, Tootsies Orchard Lounge,
Nashville, Tennessee, 1974

Opposite:
Leaving the Opry,
Grand Ole Opry,
Nashville, Tennessee, 1972

Contents

Foreword

There is an old saying that a picture is worth a thousand words. Pictures serve as reminders of what was witnessed by the photographer, which becomes a time capsule of a moment that is gone. In *Honky Tonk*, there are more than one hundred of these time-capsule moments. There aren't enough words to describe adequately such an important era in the history of country music.

The period between 1972 and 1981, when the photographs contained in this book were taken, was an exciting, yet transitional time for country music. Many of the giants of the business were at a point when their recordings, new or old, were receiving little or no airplay; a point of frustration not only for the artists but also for their longtime fans. It was a time when the "Countrypolitan" and "Nashville Sound" with background voices and string sections were reigning on recordings, when the earlier traditional stylings with large portions of steel guitar and fiddle had nearly faded away. This format was successful; as the number of radio stations programming country music grew, so did the number of new fans. The late 1970s gave way to the "Urban Cowboy" era, attracting yet another legion of new artists and fans to country music.

Henry Horenstein, a serious fan of country music, was a young Massachusetts photographer who had only been taking pictures for a few years when he made the earliest images featured in this book—individual shots of Porter Wagoner and Dolly Parton taken in Boston in 1972. Later that year, Henry made his first of three pilgrimages to Nashville. With the help of Rounder Records, then a relatively new company, for whom he was doing a shoot, Henry was able to attain backstage access to WSM's Grand Ole Opry. It was there that his camera committed to film dozens of country music greats on stage and off, in what was the Opry's last full year at the historic Mother Church of Country Music, the Ryman Auditorium. Also during the Nashville visits, Henry captured a number of wonderful images of artists at their homes, in addition to taking numerous shots at Nashville's most famous honky tonk, Tootsies Orchid Lounge.

While bluegrass music and its festivals are very popular now, these venues were in their formative years when Henry was taking his pictures. Photographs of legends like Charlie Monroe, the Blue Sky Boys, and the Bailey Brothers, all semiretired at the time, are even more legendary today to serious students of the music. Just as insightful are the youthful shots of Ricky Skaggs, then playing with J. D. Crowe, and the ultratraditional Del McCoury in front of one of his first buses.

Country music parks, once a thriving entity, especially north of the Mason-Dixon line, are virtually extinct today. Henry was in the right place at the right time to capture the images of more legends like Mother Maybelle Carter, Carl and Pearl Butler, Ernest Tubb, along with one of his most famous lead guitar players, Billy Byrd, among others.

Johnson Mountain Boys
with Eddie Stubbs (fiddle),
Larry Robbins (bass),
Richard Underwood (banjo),
David McLaughlin (mandolin),
Dudley Connell (guitar).
Hanover, Massachusetts, 1981

The chapter devoted to honky tonks is especially important to country music history. For several decades, honky tonks were a haven where a band could learn and hone its skills, try out new material, play old songs that radio didn't program anymore, and essentially learn to put on a show. Honky tonks were a tremendous training ground for a band that could learn when to get out of this environment and move up the ladder to work in better places that offered more money. Once a thriving entity for country music fans to see and hear live music as well as listen to a jukebox loaded with country records, the honky tonk is a piece of Americana that is fading quickly into obscurity, having given way to chain restaurants with fern bars. In the middle 1980s, VCRs were becoming an almost essential part of every home, and stronger DWI/DUI laws and enforcement went into effect. As a result, people started going out less and staying home more. It was a lot easier and cheaper to stay at home, put a tape in the VCR, and "pop a top" on a can of beer in the den. While these life-saving laws were essential socially, they definitely had a negative effect on live music at the time.

Billy Byrd,
Longtime Ernest Tubb guitarist,
Lone Star Ranch,
Reeds Ferry, New Hampshire, 1973

This book fills a void in the documentation of country music history, showing many venues important to the music and its patrons, who are as integral a part of the contents of this book as the performers. Through Henry's lens, we get an up-close look at these special people. Country music in those days was expanding rapidly, attracting new fans all the time, but it couldn't shake loose the longtime fans: hard-core, largely blue-collar workers who bought the Carl Smith and Kitty Wells records when they were new back in the 1950s. When you look at the images of the fans out in front of the Ryman Auditorium, the older people especially, you can tell that these were *real* country music fans. In many cases these individuals had saved for years, in some instances a lifetime, to make the journey to Nashville and see the Grand Ole Opry. These are people who knew all the words to Ernest Tubb's "Walking the Floor Over You" and George Morgan's "Candy Kisses," and could tell you the name of Loretta Lynn's latest single on the radio.

Even though it was a troubling time for our nation, with the Watergate scandal surrounding then-president Richard Nixon and other big issues that would shape America's future, it was a simpler time for country music. In the opinion of many longtime fans and observers, the 1970s were the last great decade of country music. Granted, while multitalented traditional stylists like Ricky Skaggs, Randy Travis, George Strait, Vince Gill, and Alan Jackson have all emerged since then, their legacy belongs to a different era.

This book's most recent photograph was taken in October of 1981 in Hanover, Massachusetts. The subjects were a new band on the bluegrass circuit out of Maryland, just nearing the end of their first year on the road as a full-time group. They were the Johnson Mountain Boys, an act for which I was proud to be the fiddle player for eighteen years. The photo shoot was for a new publicity picture and for an album cover for the group's second album on Rounder, entitled *Walls of Time*.

It was on this blustery, cold, autumn day that I first met Henry Horenstein. Henry had taken a number of album cover photographs for Rounder, and we were all acquainted with his work in that area. At the time, if we had gotten to see the full contents of this book, we probably would have tied him up for hours asking an endless number of questions like, "How did it feel to attend the Opry at the Ryman?," and "What was it like to photograph DeFord Bailey?"

The photographs in this book take me back to when I was a teenager in the 1970s, the early years of what for me has become an obsession with all facets of bluegrass and traditional country music. Henry's images remind me vividly what icons Ernest Tubb, Bill Monroe, and Lester Flatt looked like the first time I saw them, either on network television or in person. They, and numerous others, definitely had a different look from the musicians on the 1950s and 1960s album covers I had studied so meticulously. To keep up with the times, many male country artists were letting their hair grow longer and fuller and had let their sideburns grow down to the bottom of their ears. Hair coloring, long a staple in female grooming, was becoming common among the older male stars in country music. At the time, they were wearing polyester more often than the sequined gabardine outfits from tailors like Nudie Cohen or Manuel that had been so prevalent among country stars.

Although none of us knew it at the time, some of the artists captured in this book were in the last decade of their lives. By the 1970s, the interstate highways in most areas had only been in use for a decade. To make life easier, many of the stars had gravitated to traveling by bus. However, the rigors of the road—in many cases a lifelong unhealthy diet of foods high in cholesterol and saturated fat, often coupled with addiction to tobacco and sometimes alcohol, along with family problems, and business pressures—all contributed to the aging process, sadly, not always in a graceful manner.

Horenstein's images of the fans, standing alone or as part of the audience, and especially in the honky tonks, transport me back to the middle and late 1970s. At the time I was legally underage, playing music in some of northern-central Maryland's finest smoky roadhouse taverns. The way these patrons looked, the clothes they wore, the hair styles, the way they acted, the lifestyle they possessed, and the passion they had for the music, are wonderful memories that Henry has allowed many of us who were around at the time to call up again.

Photographs, like music, serve as memory makers. For many who look at these pages, Henry Horenstein's images will open a floodgate of memories. To those who have come to the music since the 1970s, welcome! Whether you're a lifelong fan or just got introduced to country music yesterday, this book is an absolute treasure chest of special photographs. There is much here to enjoy, not only by the artists and musicians, but by the fans who made it all possible.

—**Eddie Stubbs**
WSM Grand Ole Opry Announcer
Nashville, Tennessee

Introduction
Three Chords and the Truth

A lot of people assume that country music is a Southern thing. It isn't: it's everywhere. It always has been—even in New Bedford, Massachusetts, where I grew up, one hour south of Boston.

By the time I was eight years old, I was hanging out at New Bedford's only music store, the Melody Shop. The owner was kid-friendly, and an older guy, a folksinger named Paul Clayton, spent a lot of time there as well. Turns out there wasn't much interest in his specialty—whaling songs— except in New Bedford, which in the nineteenth century was one of the world's great whaling ports.

Clayton did help rearrange an old folksong called "Gotta Travel On," which became a big hit for country singer Billy Grammer in 1959. Bob Dylan covered it years later in his *Self Portrait* album. But before Clayton had to travel on—and out—of our hometown, he recommended my very first LP purchase: *Johnny Cash Sings Hank Williams* on Sun Records. I still play that record. Although it was a style of music with which I was already familiar, no one ever told me it was country music.

Mainstream radio stations in the mid-to-late 1950s commonly programmed country music. Only they didn't call it that. Country was equated with hillbilly and few stations wanted that association. The audience for country music was thought to be too limited and too poor. Better to play Pat Boone, Johnny Mathis, and the new rock-and-roll, which was essentially a hybrid of country music and rhythm-and-blues. The demographics were better—the audience was younger and had more disposable income—and this allowed higher advertising rates to be charged.

Take Elvis Presley, for example. Elvis grew up poor in Tupelo, Mississippi. He played gospel and country music and eventually became fond of the blues. He melded all these styles and made music history—and a ton of money. After that, record companies went looking for white country singers with a little rhythm. Maybe, they thought they could find another Elvis.

Another Elvis was too much to hope for. But there were quite a few good old boys, and even a couple of good old girls, who rode the airwaves in the late 1950s. And they were my favorites: Johnny Cash (of course), Marty Robbins, Jerry Lee Lewis, Johnny Horton, Wanda Jackson,

Stonewall Jackson, Skeeter Davis, and Jimmie Rodgers (the other one, not the legendary "Singing Brakeman" of the 1920s and '30s).

The late songwriter Harlan Howard was once asked what made a great county song. "Three chords and the truth," he answered. He would know. Howard wrote Patsy Cline's great hit "I Fall to Pieces," as well as "Busted" (Ray Charles), "Heartaches by the Number" (Ray Price), "Tiger by the Tail" (Buck Owens, who was also cowriter), and so many other country classics.

What he meant by "three chords" was simplicity, and I understood that from listening to folk music, much of which can be faked on guitar if you know D, G, and A7. When I was in high school, my parents moved us from New Bedford to Boston, and I spent many more nights at Cambridge's legendary Club 47 than at my new home. In a single week at the "47," you might see bluesmen like Muddy Waters and bluegrass bands like the Kentucky Colonels. Though folk songs and country music aren't exactly the same thing, there are deep connections. Many times at the "47" I saw Jim Kweskin and the Jug Band with Bill Keith, who revolutionized bluegrass banjo while working with the legendary Bill Monroe. I first heard Johnny Cash's plaintive "I Still Miss Someone" and Lefty Frizzell's classic "Long Black Veil" from the singing of Joan Baez.

I suspect by "truth" Howard meant directness and honesty. But to me, it meant something else. I was a determined student of history in high school and college, and much of the folk and country tradition is narrative, describing stories and events often historical or legendary in nature. Certainly Woody Guthrie's music, as in a song like "Pretty Boy Floyd," falls into this category, as does so much of country music: Marty Robbins's "Big Iron," Johnny Cash's "Folsom Prison Blues," and Johnny Horton's "The Battle of New Orleans" come to mind. And even today, I don't know of a more eloquent reminiscence of the events of September 11, 2001, than Alan Jackson's "Where Were You (When the World Stopped Turning?)."

I studied history at the University of Chicago and had several great teachers there. One of them, Jesse Lemisch, introduced me to the work of the noted English historian E.P. Thompson, whom I later studied with at the University of Warwick. I learned many things from these teachers that I tried to apply to my photography. One was that there is no pure "truth"; what you read depends very much on the point of view of the teller—or the historian. And I learned that the points of view of "successful" people and cultures were the ones most remembered. These successful types were the ones who were in the best position to write down and record what they accomplished, what they felt, and what they believed in.

LEFT:
Stonewall Jackson, backstage at the Grand Ole Opry, Nashville, Tennessee, 1972

RIGHT:
Bill Keith (on banjo) with the Jim Kweskin Jug Band, Newport Folk Festival, Newport, Rhode Island, 1967

I translated this understanding to what I knew about music. I concluded that if I were interested in studying about truckers, for example, wouldn't I rather listen to Dave Dudley's "Six Days on the Road" than a speech by the Secretary of Transportation?

> *It seems like a month*
> *Since I kissed my baby goodbye.*
> *I could have a lot of women*
> *But I'm not like some other guys.*
> *I could find someone to hold me tight*
> *But I could never make believe it's all right.*
> *Six days on the road and I'm gonna make it home tonight.*

"Six Days on the Road," BY EARL GREEN AND CARL C. MONTGOMERY

In my junior year in college I became interested in photography. For one thing, it got me out of the library stacks and involved me with people rather than with books. And honestly, photography was "cooler" than history, and it got me a lot more dates. But I always kept what I learnt as a historian in mind as I tried to figure out how to make the uncertain transition from academic to artist.

Photographer Danny Lyons, at that time a recent history graduate of the University of Chicago, had just made that transition, publishing his landmark photoessay *The Bikeriders*, about the Outlaw motorcycle club in Chicago. I saw him as a historian with a camera. And that's what I wanted to be.

I also became familiar with the work of Robert Frank, Lyons's predecessor, who produced one of the greatest photography books ever, *The Americans*. (I was gratified when I heard Frank lecture years later to hear him say that his favorite musician was Hank Williams.) And of course before Frank there were other terrific examples of fine (artistic) documentary photographers whose pictures worked well with text and in books: Walker Evans, who produced *Let Us Now Praise Famous Men* (with text by James Agee), and Dorothea Lange's *An American Exodus* (with Paul Taylor).

So I knew that I wanted to take pictures, make books, and record history. But where to start? A few years later, my photography teacher at the Rhode Island School of Design, Harry Callahan, answered the question simply by telling me to photograph people and places to which I was naturally drawn. In his way, Callahan was saying the same thing as Harlan Howard: Be true to yourself. How could I have missed that? And so I started photographing even more around music shows and concerts. I figured that even if I got lousy pictures, I would probably have a good time.

Fiddler Mack Magaha,
at home, Nashville, Tennessee, 1974

I finished my art training in 1973 and set out to apply what I had learned. In those days there was very little hope of making a living as a documentary photographer. So I took a variety of jobs, not all in photography, and took pictures on the side. Rounder Records was starting out about this time and I did some work for them—usually publicity and album covers. I also photographed a little for magazines such as *Country Music, Bluegrass Unlimited,* and *Muleskinner News.* But mostly I photographed for myself.

I drove to Nashville a few times with friends and stopped on the way to photograph Ralph Stanley and Curly Ray Cline. In Nashville, I took photographs at the Ryman Auditorium during the Grand Ole Opry shows and at the legendary Tootsies Orchid Lounge. And when possible, I went to the homes of performers who were gracious enough to invite me in—Wilma Lee and Stoney Cooper, Mack Magaha, and Del Reeves.

Almost every summer Sunday for years I went to the Lone Star Ranch, a country music park in southern New Hampshire. There I saw and photographed legendary acts like Ernest Tubb and Mother Maybelle Carter. And I went to bluegrass festivals. In Pennsylvania I photographed a young Del McCoury and the elderly Blue Sky Boys, and in Maryland I shot legends Charlie Monroe and John Duffey.

Then there were the honky tonks—slightly disreputable bars with live music. In Boston, we had the Hillbilly Ranch and I photographed Tex Ritter there, as well as regular patrons, such as Hillbilly Tex, who was neither a hillbilly nor from Texas. I also photographed in bars that played country music wherever I could—quite a few in Louisiana, in particular, since I was dating a girl from New Orleans.

All along, in my historian's mind, I saw all this as a disappearing world that I wanted to preserve on film. As I look back, many years later, it's sad to see that I wasn't far off. Many of the people and the places pictured here are long gone, though some have adjusted and survived. There are still bluegrass festivals, but the Grand Ole Opry is no longer based at the Ryman Auditorium. Tootsies Orchid Lounge lives on in a smaller room, but the Hillbilly Ranch and so many lesser honky tonks do not. There are hardly any country music parks left. And we've lost so many great musicians, naturally, and along with them went a way of life. Everyone will remember Elvis Presley and the Beatles, but I wonder: Will they remember Kitty Wells, Ernest Tubb, or, for that matter, Hillbilly Tex? These pictures were made in hopes that they will.

Who's gonna fill their shoes
Who's gonna stand that tall
Who's gonna play the Opry
And the Wabash Cannonball
Who's gonna give their heart and soul
To get to me and you
Lord I wonder, who's gonna fill their shoes?

"Who's Gonna Fill Their Shoes?" BY TROY SEALS AND MAX D. BARNES

13

People Like You

Fans listen to country music in clubs, on the radio, and sometimes on television. But perhaps the biggest commitment they can make to the music is to pile into their car, pickup, or RV and go to a live show, whether it's in a concert hall or on a tiny village green. That's because touring and playing live is the primary means for most country acts to earn money and stay active. Only the megastars make big money from record sales.

There are two venues where country music really rules: country-music parks and bluegrass festivals. Music parks became popular in the 1940s and 1950s as summer gathering places for families. Many, such as Lone Star Ranch, Indian Ranch, and Take It Easy Ranch, had Wild West themes. Some music parks had a lake for swimming by day and a bar for dancing by night. Others had a restaurant on the premises, but most families barbecued their own meals. And on Sunday afternoons there would be entertainment—maybe a kids' show, but almost certainly a country music band.

While a few remain, most county-music parks are long gone, victims of real-estate development and changing demographics and musical tastes. But bluegrass festivals are still very popular—more than five hundred are listed in the annual festival guide in *Bluegrass Unlimited* magazine. Although the first festivals started in the 1960s, they became especially popular in the 1970s. And while bluegrass music is in the spotlight, a few of these festivals also feature old-time traditional music of all kinds—folk, country, Irish, Cajun, and so on.

Perhaps the most notable thing about bluegrass festivals is that they have helped preserve the music by providing a place for traditional musicians to work and for their fans to hear them. But another important contribution is that bluegrass festivals have brought together disparate fans—young and old, urban and rural, rich and poor, educated and not—whose only obvious connection is the music.

The Blue Sky Boys,
Sunday Morning Gospel Show,
Gettysburg Bluegrass Festival,
Gettysburg, Pennsylvania, 1974

Fans surrounding Ernest Tubb

LONE STAR RANCH. REEDS FERRY. NEW HAMPSHIRE. 1973

Tommy Cash, Johnny's brother, signing autographs

LONE STAR RANCH. REEDS FERRY. NEW HAMPSHIRE. 1973

Dancing to Webb Pierce
LONE STAR RANCH, REEDS FERRY, NEW HAMPSHIRE, 1972

Fans photographing their daughter with Carl and Pearl Butler

LONE STAR RANCH, REEDS FERRY, NEW HAMPSHIRE, 1973

Bluegrass music fan Frank Brown
GETTYSBURG BLUEGRASS FESTIVAL. GETTYSBURG. PENNSYLVANIA. 1974

Tom Taylor, brother of bluegrass musician Earl Taylor

GETTYSBURG BLUEGRASS FESTIVAL. GETTYSBURG. PENNSYLVANIA. 1974

Ernest Tubb and fans
LONE STAR RANCH, REEDS FERRY, NEW HAMPSHIRE, 1973

Concession stand

LONE STAR RANCH, REEDS FERRY, NEW HAMPSHIRE, 1972

Country music fan
LONE STAR RANCH, REEDS FERRY, NEW HAMPSHIRE, 1972

Bluegrass music fans
BERRYVILLE BLUEGRASS FESTIVAL, BERRYVILLE, VIRGINIA, 1974

Playground
LONE STAR RANCH. REEDS FERRY. NEW HAMPSHIRE. 1975

Banjo pickin' dog

GETTYSBURG BLUEGRASS FESTIVAL. GETTYSBURG. PENNSYLVANIA. 1974

Fiddler Clarence "Tater" Tate

BERRYVILLE BLUEGRASS FESTIVAL. BERRYVILLE. VIRGINIA. 1974

Webb Pierce's Bonneville
LONE STAR RANCH, REEDS FERRY, NEW HAMPSHIRE, 1973

The Mother Church

The heyday of radio was the 1930s and 1940s, before television took over the hearts and minds of Americans. As fledgling stations in the 1920s were looking for programming, many turned to traditional music to satisfy the mostly rural audiences of that era. In Nashville, WSM (for "We Shield Millions," the slogan of the National Life and Accident Insurance Company, which owned the station) hired the "Solemn Old Judge" George D. Hay to run things. He introduced the Opry as a live radio show of traditional instrumental music in 1925.

The show grew in popularity, and in the 1930s, really took off. In 1932, WSM received a license to broadcast at fifty-thousand watts, the maximum allowed by the FCC. This gave the Opry a huge audience, ranging from all over the South and much of the Midwest to other parts of the country and North America as well. In 1939, NBC added thirty minutes of the Opry to its network programming, significantly broadening its reach and influence.

More listeners over a broader geographical area meant more opportunity for touring performers who made their money by playing live shows, not by selling records, which were just starting to be distributed widely. This broad exposure attracted star talent to the Opry. While the acts that came in the 1930s were "country" in the broadest sense, they were actually quite different musically. Pee Wee King's Golden West Cowboys, a Western pop-country band, came in 1937; Roy Acuff and the Smoky Mountain Boys, a crooning hillbilly act, in 1938; Bill Monroe with his jazzed-up mountain music, later called bluegrass music after the name of his band, the Blue Grass Boys, in 1939; and Minnie Pearl, the consummate hayseed comedienne, in 1940.

The Opry had several homes as its audience grew. The Opry finally settled at the Ryman Auditorium, called the "Mother Church of Country Music," on Fifth Avenue North, off lower Broadway, in 1943. The show stayed at the Ryman until March 15, 1974—around the time many of these pictures were made— and was then moved to Opryland, a large theme park and hotel complex on the outskirts of Nashville, where it remains active and influential.

Waiting in Line (1),
Grand Ole Opry,
Nashville, Tennessee, 1972

Waiting in line (2)
GRAND OLE OPRY, NASHVILLE, TENNESSEE, 1974

Waiting in line (3)
GRAND OLE OPRY, NASHVILLE, TENNESSEE, 1974

Cates Sisters
GRAND OLE OPRY. NASHVILLE. TENNESSEE. 1972

The Willis Brothers
GRAND OLE OPRY. NASHVILLE. TENNESSEE. 1972

Fiddlin' Sid Harkreader

GRAND OLE OPRY. NASHVILLE. TENNESSEE. 1974

Lonzo and Oscar

GRAND OLE OPRY, NASHVILLE, TENNESSEE, 1972

Acme Boots representative, sponsor of show
GRAND OLE OPRY, NASHVILLE, TENNESSEE, 1972

Bashful Brother Oswald
GRAND OLE OPRY. NASHVILLE. TENNESSEE. 1972

Waiting backstage
GRAND OLE OPRY. NASHVILLE. TENNESSEE. 1972

Carol Lee Cooper backstage
GRAND OLE OPRY, NASHVILLE, TENNESSEE, 1974

Hey buddy bring me a beer
Somebody's playing my song
That's why I like it in here.
I feel I really belong.
And the waitresses always treat me right
When I get a little too loud
I like hangin' around in a honky tonk crowd.

"Honky Tonk Crowd," BY LIONEL A. DELMORE
AND LARRY CORDLE

Honky Tonkin'

Country music, alcohol, tobacco, and cheating love mix well. If you don't believe it, listen to the songs. "Prop Me Up Beside the Jukebox (If I Die)," "Smoke! Smoke! Smoke! (That Cigarette)," "It Was Always So Easy (To Find an Unhappy Woman)," "Straight Tequila Night," "Six Pack to Go," "There's a Tear in My Beer," "Dim Lights, Thick Smoke (and Loud, Loud Music)."

The term "honky tonk" strictly refers to the type of bar that became popular after prohibition ended in the mid-1930s—a place that was at least a little seedy and usually located on the outskirts of town—away from churches, schools, and God-fearing folks. At a typical honky tonk, one could find live music, alcohol, romance, divorce, friendship, and brawling—and the amplified music of Hank Williams, Lefty Frizzell, and Hank Thompson.

Of course, there are still a lot of bars that fit this description. But the heyday of the honky tonk ended in the early to mid-1960s with the arrival of the jukebox and recorded music. Country bars today are more likely to be civilized affairs where couples line dance politely with each other and don't actually have affairs. In fact, you'd be hard-pressed to find reference to alcohol, smoking, or cheating in most modern country songs—at least the songs you hear on mainstream country radio.

Many people think of honky tonks as a Southern institution. Not at all. They were everywhere. The photographs here are from different parts of the country, including the Hillbilly Ranch in Boston, located on the edge of the notorious Combat Zone, adjacent to the Continental Bus Terminal. The Lilly Brothers (with Don Stover) from Clear Creek, West Virginia, was the house band for the Hillbilly Ranch for eighteen years (1952–1970). On a given night, you might find sailors from the Charlestown Naval Yard, shipworkers from the Quincy Fore River Shipyard, off-duty bus drivers certainly, secretaries from the Financial District, and slumming college students. Johnny Cash played there, as did Kitty Wells, Little Jimmy Dickens, Tex Ritter, and many others—most of whom are long forgotten.

Harmonica player,
Merchant's Cafe,
Nashville, Tennessee, 1974

Wall behind the bar

TOOTSIES ORCHID LOUNGE, NASHVILLE, TENNESSEE, 1974

Dancing
FRED'S LOUNGE, MAMOU, LOUISIANA, 1977

Hillbilly Tex
HILLBILLY RANCH. BOSTON. MASSACHUSETTS. 1972

Patron

HILLBILLY RANCH. BOSTON. MASSACHUSETTS. 1972

Lilly Brothers reunion show
HILLBILLY RANCH, BOSTON, MASSACHUSETTS, 1978

Friends in booths
FRED'S LOUNGE, MAMOU, LOUISIANA, 1977

Listening to the band

HILLBILLY RANCH, BOSTON, MASSACHUSETTS, 1978

Patrons at a honky tonk
LAFAYETTE. LOUISIANA. 1977

At the bar
FRED'S LOUNGE, MAMOU, LOUISIANA, 1977

Dewey Balfa of the Balfa Brothers Band
BEARCAT LOUNGE, BASILE, LOUISIANA, 1977

Tootsies Orchid Lounge

Founded in 1960, and still located on lower Broadway across the alley (thirty-seven steps) from the back door of the Ryman Auditorium, Tootsies Orchid Lounge is one of Nashville treasures, a relic from the pre-Opryland days. But times have changed since 1974 when the Opry left the Ryman for that theme park. In days past, musicians could stop in between sets to say hi, have a beer, and meet their fans up close and personal.

We're told that Kris Kristofferson swept floors at Tootsies while shopping "Me and Bobby McGee" around. Burt Reynolds filmed part of *W. W. & the Dixie Dance Kings* there. This is the place where Faron Young hired a young Roger Miller to play drums in his band, though Roger had never played drums before. Tom T. Hall drank vats of beer at Tootsies, trading stories with fellow "Outlaws" Kristofferson, Waylon Jennings, Bobby Bare, Tompall Glaser, Billy Joe Shaver, and Willie Nelson. And, yes, it was there that Willie wrote "Crazy" for Patsy Cline, and convinced Faron to record his "Hello Walls" at a side table with the help of his friend Johnny Walker.

There are so many great stories, and some of them are almost certainly true.

What we know is true is that scores of wannabe country singers and songwriters from all over the world made Tootsies their first stop in Nashville, hoping to find someone—anyone—to listen to their songs. Every night Hattie Louise Tatum Bess, a.k.a. Tootsie, would sell them beer, put their demo 45s on her jukebox, slip them a $5 bill if they looked like they needed it, and finally, at closing time, kick them all out with her trademark whistle. When that didn't work, she used a knitting needle, given to her by superstar Country Charlie Pride, to poke hearing-impaired drinkers out the door.

Tootsie's death in 1978 marked the end of an era as surely as when the Grand Ole Opry left the Ryman for Opryland. In her later years, she was fond of saying to anyone who would listen, "The Opry left me, I didn't leave the Opry."

Tootsie at closing time,
Tootsies Orchid Lounge,
Nashville, Tennessee, 1974

Wall
TOOTSIES ORCHID LOUNGE. NASHVILLE. TENNESSEE. 1972

Jukebox
TOOTSIES ORCHID LOUNGE. NASHVILLE. TENNESSEE. 1972

Booth
TOOTSIES ORCHID LOUNGE. NASHVILLE. TENNESSEE. 1974

Music fans
TOOTSIES ORCHID LOUNGE. NASHVILLE. TENNESSEE. 1974

House band

TOOTSIES ORCHID LOUNGE. NASHVILLE. TENNESSEE. 1974

Lovers
TOOTSIES ORCHID LOUNGE. NASHVILLE. TENNESSEE. 1975

Bartender
TOOTSIES ORCHID LOUNGE. NASHVILLE. TENNESSEE. 1974

Playing for tips

TOOTSIES ORCHID LOUNGE. NASHVILLE. TENNESSEE. 1974

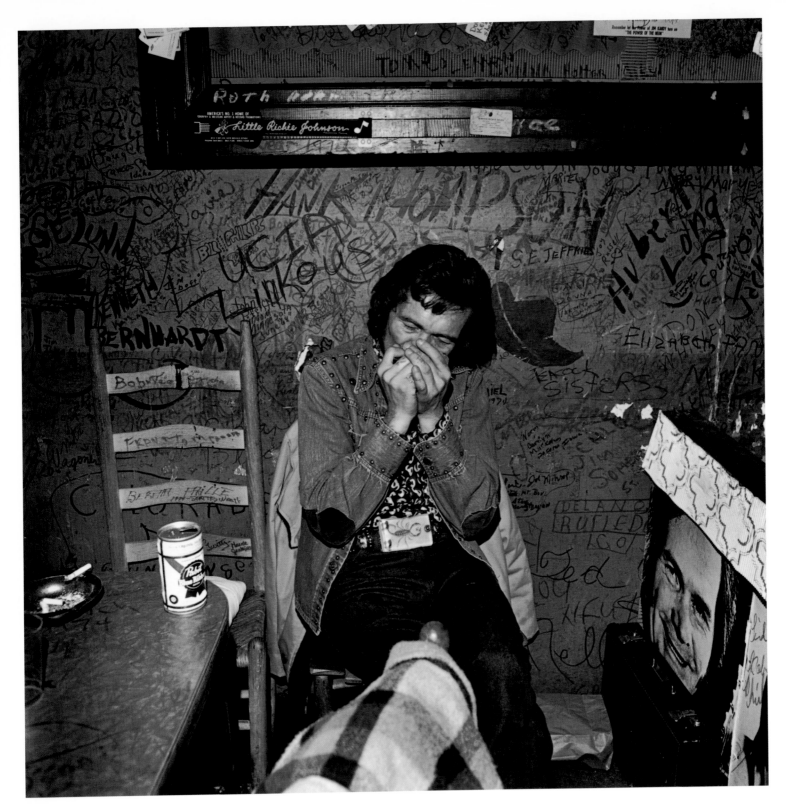

Pitching a song

TOOTSIES ORCHID LOUNGE. NASHVILLE. TENNESSEE. 1974

Last call
TOOTSIES ORCHID LOUNGE, NASHVILLE, TENNESSEE, 1974

Pickin' and Singin'

Country musicians are first and foremost entertainers. They write, play, and sing the songs their fans want to hear. And for the few who are successful, there is stardom, recognition—and maybe even wealth. Fans attach so much glamour to the profession that it's sometimes hard to keep in mind that musicians are working people, trying hard to put bread on the table. For every Faith Hill and Garth Brooks, there are tens of thousands of musicians waiting tables and waiting for a break.

The earliest country musicians didn't tour. They made their reputations locally. With radio came the opportunity to spread the word for record sales but particularly for live shows. A band could tour out the areas reached by whatever radio station featured them. Television brought more and better opportunities. Today's country stars fly first class to their shows and a caravan of buses follow with their supporting crew, instruments, computers, and audio-visual equipment.

Country stars of the 1970s for the most part traveled lean. Even for successful acts, one old bus usually fit all. And the most employable bass players were better mechanics than musicians; someone had to keep that bus cranking and on the road.

A few stars did well enough to put their band on salary, but that might mean painting fences and planting crops for their boss between paying gigs. Even well-known acts struggled. Not Roy Acuff certainly, but he made real money in the music publishing business, not by touring out. For a while, even legend Mother Maybelle Carter worked part-time by day as a practical nurse in an old-age home, and then played the Opry at night.

The glamour was there for the fans to see. Performers dressed in rhinestone suits and signed autographs for everyone who asked. But it was also a tough life and many paid the price in substance abuse, unstable families, and often early death. But for the few who made it, it was a dream come true. Just like in the movies.

Ramona and Grandpa Jones (page 66)

GRAND OLE OPRY, NASHVILLE, TENNESSEE, 1974

Grandpa Jones was best known for his work on the Grand Ole Opry, starting in 1946, and *Hee Haw*, often performing with his wife, Ramona. Born Louis Marshall Jones, he actually started playing the part of a grandpa in 1935, at the ripe age of 22, teaming up with traditional singer Bradley Kincaid to work the popular *Lum and Abner* radio show broadcast from (of all places) Boston. The act worked well enough that Jones remained a grandpa until he died in 1998. One of the best of the old-time banjo players, balladeers, and comedians, Jones suffered a stroke on the Opry stage. As cast members gathered around him, he looked up and said, "Well, I guess I can still draw a crowd."

Mother Maybelle Carter

LONE STAR RANCH, REEDS FERRY, NEW HAMPSHIRE, 1973

The Carter Family (Maybelle, her cousin Sara, and Sara's husband and Maybelle's husband's brother A.P.) was one of the foundation acts of country music. Their story is legendary, beginning with their first recordings in Bristol, Tennessee, in 1927, the same session that introduced the "Singing Brakeman" Jimmie Rodgers. Songs they popularized became country music classics, from "Wildwood Flower" to "Will the Circle Be Unbroken?" And you can still hear Mother Maybelle's patented single-note guitar style in many folk, country, and even rock-and-roll recordings. That's daughter Helen on the accordion.

Porter Wagoner (page 70)

SYMPHONY HALL, BOSTON, MASSACHUSETTS, 1972

Porter Wagoner has long been the quintessential country entertainer, combining sharp outfits with old-time country humor and a lively band. Perhaps best known for his association with Dolly Parton—she was a member of his band and a duet-recording partner from 1967 to 1974—Porter was a huge country star well before Dolly came along, and long after. His first big hit was in 1954 ("Company's Coming") and his songs continued charting well into the 1980s. *The Porter Wagoner Show*, an early syndicated television show (1960–1980), had more than 100 subscriber stations at its peak.

Dolly Parton (page 71)

SYMPHONY HALL, BOSTON, MASSACHUSETTS, 1972

Dolly's first hit was "Dumb Blonde" in 1967, but she soon proved she was anything but. She worked in the popular Porter Wagoner band from 1967 to 1974, then moved on to multiple careers in music, film (*9 to 5*), and business (Dollywood, the theme park). Her musical style went pop and her show became more Vegas than Nashville, and she continued writing hit songs, including "I Will Always Love You," recorded by Whitney Houston in 1992. Today, Dolly has returned to her roots, singing and writing traditional music in a simple, unadorned style, which most feel best shows off her considerable talents.

Hank Williams Jr.

LONE STAR RANCH, REEDS FERRY, NEW HAMPSHIRE, 1973

Son of the most famous country singers ever, Hank Jr. went into the family business early; he was already a seasoned performer when he first played on the Grand Ole Opry at age thirteen. A few years later, he recorded the plaintive "Standing in the Shadow (of a Very Famous Man)," which might well have served as the epitaph on his tombstone. However, Junior proved to have considerable staying power as a singer, songwriter, and entertainer. Melding his dad's honky tonk sound with a scoop of Southern rock, he has had dozens of hit records and awards of his own, but might be best known for singing the opening theme for ABC's *Monday Night Football*.

Minnie Pearl and Pee Wee King

GRAND OLE OPRY, NASHVILLE, TENNESSEE, 1973

Minnie was the preeminent country comedian of her day—arguably any day. With a $1.98 price tag hanging from her hat, she greeted her audience with an unmistakable "How-dee," and regaled them with corny tales about the citizens of Grinder's Switch, influencing among others Garrison Keillor (and his tales of Lake Wobegon). Born Sarah Ophelia Colley, Minnie was a member of the Grand Ole Opry from 1940 until her death in 1996. She also was a cast member of the popular *Hee Haw* television show.

Pee Wee King was a pop/country accordion player who fronted a big band that at various times employed (among others) Country Music Hall of Famers Eddy Arnold and Minnie Pearl. Although he had a long career, beginning in the early 1930s, he is best remembered for the songs he is credited with writing or co-writing: "Bonaparte's Retreat," "Slow Poke," and "Tennessee Waltz"—one of the state songs of Tennessee, a no. 1 pop hit for Patti Page in 1950, and one of the most recorded songs of all time.

Tex Ritter
HILLBILLY RANCH. BOSTON. MASSACHUSETTS. 1973

In the 1930s and 1940s, Ritter was a successful "singing cowboy" in the same tradition as rivals Gene Autry and Roy Rogers. Like other singing cowboys, he had a multilayered career—as a film star (he made many dozens of B-Westerns), recording artist, and touring musician. Father of actor John Ritter, Tex sang "Do Not Forsake Me Oh My Darling," the theme song of *High Noon*, Gary Cooper's Academy Award–winning movie of 1953. Tex also charted with the maudlin "Deck of Cards" (1948) and oddly less maudlin "I Dreamed of a Hillbilly Heaven" (1961). Tex's dream came true when he died in early 1974, a few months after this photograph was taken.

Loretta Lynn (page 78)
BACKSTAGE. ANNAPOLIS. MARYLAND. 1975

There have been few country stars as popular and as loved as the "Coal Miner's Daughter." Lynn's fans lived her life along with her—an ongoing soap opera that included enduring a childhood of poverty, achieving a dramatic rise to stardom, and fighting depression. There was a movie about her life in 1980 with Sissy Spacek in the starring role. And Lynn had dozens of top-ten hits, many of which she wrote herself, such as "Don't Come Home a Drinkin' (with Lovin' on Your Mind)," "Your Squaw is on the Warpath," "You Ain't Woman Enough (to Take My Man)" and, of course, her signature "Coal Miner's Daughter."

Conway Twitty (page 79)
BACKSTAGE. ANNAPOLIS. MARYLAND. 1975

Born Harold Jenkins, Twitty began his career as a rockabilly singer in the Elvis Presley mold and, in 1958, had a huge pop hit "It's Only Make Believe." He switched to straight country music in the mid-1960s, and for more than two decades had dozens of top-ten country hits and more no. 1 songs than anyone in the history of country music. Playing up his reputation as a sex symbol, Twitty's bluesy baritone targeted his female fans and many of his songs featured thinly disguised sexual innuendo, such as "Tight Fittin' Jeans," "You've Never Been This Far Before," and a cover of the Pointer Sisters' "Slow Hand."

Jerry Lee Lewis
RAMADA INN. BOSTON. MASSACHUSETTS. 1975

Jerry Lee, a.k.a. "The Killer," is in the Rock-and-Roll Hall of Fame, but his roots are deep country and his life pure soap opera. He set his stage piano on fire, married his thirteen-year-old cousin, and endured health problems and family tragedies. The story was well told in 1989's *Great Balls of Fire*, with Dennis Quaid as The Killer. After his rock career died, Lewis was a constant presence on the country charts in the 1960s and 1970s, with songs that sound much like his life: "What's Made Milwaukee Famous (Has Made a Loser Out of Me)," "She Still Comes Around (to Love What's Left of Me)," "There Must be More to Life Than This."

Curly Ray Cline (page 82)
AT HOME. ROCK HOUSE. KENTUCKY. 1974

Curly Ray, pictured here with his hunting dogs, played fiddle for Ralph Stanley and the Clinch Mountain Boys for much of his career. His style was simple and precise, a perfect match for the Stanley old-time sound. Though he was a great fiddler, it was Curly Ray's showmanship that was his biggest asset. He was a livewire on stage and off, greeting fans and selling records and souvenir key chains. Curly Ray once turned down the Rolling Stones' request to play fiddle on their song "Honky Tonk Woman," because, "If people bought that record, they wouldn't buy mine."

Ralph Stanley (page 83)
AT HOME. COEBURN. VIRGINIA. 1974

Among fans of bluegrass music, Stanley stands just slightly below the mighty Bill Monroe in importance and popularity—and his legend continues to grow. Starting out in 1946 with his brother Carter, as the Stanley Brothers, he regrouped after Carter's death in 1966, becoming a favorite on the emerging folk circuit. This new audience helped preserve the band and the unique old-time mountain sound. In 2001, "Dr. Ralph" won the Grammy Award for best male vocal performance for his "O Death," a traditional tune from the soundtrack of the film *O Brother Where Art Thou?* Ralph was seventy-four years old and had never won a Grammy before. In fact, he had never even had a hit record.

Blue Sky Boys
GETTYSBURG BLUEGRASS FESTIVAL. GETTYSBURG. PENNSYLVANIA. 1974

Brother acts have long been popular in country music and Bill and Earl Bolick formed one of the most influential ever. With tight harmony singing, accompanied by a simple guitar and mandolin, the Bolick's sound can be heard clearly in such groups as the classic country act the Louvin Brothers and Rock-and-Roll Hall of Fame members the Everly Brothers. The Blue Sky Boys were active from the mid-1930s to the early 1950s, when changing styles caught up with them and they retired from full-time touring and took jobs at the post office. This photograph was taken at one of their rare reunions.

Tammy Wynette (page 86)
SKATING RINK, WALTHAM, MASSACHUSETTS, 1974

Country singers often live soap-opera-like personal lives and no one typifies this more than Tammy Wynette. She was a part-time beautician, had major hit songs, married and divorced megastar George Jones, and constantly battled severe health problems, which eventually killed her in 1998 at age fifty-seven. Tammy was best known for "Stand by Your Man," Hillary Clinton's least favorite song. Other hits included "Your Good Girl's Gonna Go Bad," "I Don't Wanna Play House," and "D-I-V-O-R-C-E," as well as memorable duets with George Jones, such as "Golden Ring" and "We're Gonna Hold On."

George Jones (page 87)
PARADISE CLUB, BOSTON, MASSACHUSETTS, 1981

One of the greatest voices in country music, the hard-living Jones is also one of its greatest rascals. Known as "No Show" for his inability to keep his concert dates—the stories of what he did instead are legend—Jones has since cleaned up his act and maintains an active touring and recording schedule well into his sixth decade as a major star. His huge output includes novelty songs ("White Lightning"), love songs ("Walk Through This World with Me"), and the maudlin ("He Stopped Loving Her Today," about a friend who just died)—all rendered with heartfelt emotion and soul. He has also recorded duets with Ray Charles, Elvis Costello, Linda Ronstadt, and James Taylor, who wrote and sang on Jones's 1978 hit "Bartender's Blues."

Connie Smith
GRAND OLE OPRY, NASHVILLE, TENNESSEE, 1972

Dubbed "Cute and Country" and the "Sweetheart of the Grand Ole Opry," Connie Smith had one of the strongest female voices in country music in the 1960s and 1970s. She was discovered by "Whisperin'" Bill Anderson and had a no. 1 hit in 1964 with her first effort, Anderson's "Once a Day." Smith continued to score with both heartbreakers ("Ain't Had No Lovin'") and hopeful tunes ("The Hurtin's All Over"). Strongly religious, Smith turned toward gospel music in the late 1970s, before returning to her secular music, sounding and looking pretty much the same as she did when her songs were charting years ago. In 1997, she married country star and heartthrob Marty Stuart.

Del McCoury

GETTYSBURG BLUEGRASS FESTIVAL. GETTYSBURG. PENNSLYVANIA. 1974

Some entertainers reach stardom at a young age; for others, it's a long process. Delano Floyd McCoury is a good example of the latter. In the 1950s he played bluegrass part-time in the bars of Baltimore, then landed a job singing and playing guitar for Bill Monroe in 1963. Del formed the Dixie Pals in the late 1960s and the Del McCoury Band in the early 1990s, and he quietly became one of the top acts in the business, mixing an incredible tenor voice with a pure traditional sound and strong contemporary material. Along the way, his collaborators and showmates have included the rock band Phish and alt-country star Steve Earle, as well as sons and band members Ronnie on mandolin and Robbie on banjo.

Waylon Jennings (page 92)

PERFORMANCE CENTER. CAMBRIDGE. MASSACHUSETTS. 1975

No one personified the hard-living, honky tonk life the way that Waylon did. Born in Littlefield, Texas, in 1937, he played bass with rock-and-roll legend Buddy Holly in the 1950s, roomed and misbehaved with Johnny Cash in the 1960s, and had dozens of top-ten hits along the way—including 1978's "Mama Don't Let Your Babies Grow Up to Be Cowboys." But it was as an "Outlaw" that Waylon made his biggest contribution. Along with co-conspirators Willie Nelson, Tompall Glaser, Billy Joe Shaver, and others, the Outlaws streamlined arrangements, eschewed clichéd lyrics, and modernized country music by looking back to its soulful roots and mixing in a shot of rock-and-roll.

Anne Murray (page 93)

PERFORMANCE CENTER. CAMBRIDGE. MASSACHUSETTS. 1974

Dubbed the "Canadian Songbird," Murray was a physical education teacher turned performer from Nova Scotia. Her easy listening sound with a bit of folk music thrown in competed with the raw "Outlaw" sounds of Willie Nelson and Waylon Jennings for radio airplay throughout the 1970s and 1980s. Her first hit, "Snowbird," went gold in 1970, climbing to the top of the pop and country charts. From there, Murray alternated between Las Vegas and Nashville in style, with dozens of hits, including the movie soundtrack "Could I Have this Dance?" from 1980's *Urban Cowboy*, and 1984's "Nobody Loves Me Like You Do," a duet with Dave Loggins.

Don Stover

AT HOME. BILLERICA. MASSACHUSETTS. 1972

Stover was a bluegrass banjo picker from White Oak, West Virginia. He came to Boston in 1952 with the Lilly Brothers from nearby Clear Creek and they played together for over eighteen years at Boston's Hillbilly Ranch and other venues. As the first bluegrass banjo player of note in the area, he had immeasurable impact on a generation of important young pickers. Stover influenced Bill Keith, who popularized chromatic scales to bluegrass as a member of Bill Monroe's band, and Bela Fleck, a bluegrass and jazz-fusion star. This photograph was the cover of Stover's first LP for the fledgling Rounder record label.

Norman Blake (page 96)
PICKIN' PARLOR. NASHVILLE. TENNESSEE. 1974

Blake has long been one of our best and busiest traditional musicians. He played in Johnny Cash's band in the 1960s, backed up Bob Dylan on his influential *Nashville Skyline* album (1969), teamed with the late John Hartford, Vassar Clements, Randy Scruggs, and Tut Taylor in some of the most innovative recordings combining "old" and "new" bluegrass in the 1970s, and was featured on two of the most influential collections albums—Nitty Gritty Dirt Band's *Will the Circle Be Unbroken?* (1972), and the more recent film soundtrack *O Brother Where Art Thou?* (2001). Over the years, Blake has emerged as a solo act and in duet with his cellist wife Nancy, sporting an understated voice to match his unadorned guitar style.

Doc Watson (page 97)
PERFORMANCE CENTER. CAMBRIDGE. MASSACHUSETTS. 1974

A blind guitarist and singer from Deep Gap, North Carolina, Watson made his reputation as a folk singer, after his discovery in 1961 by folklorist Ralph Rinzler. His music is a combination of styles—pop, blues, folk, and old-time country—with a unique fast and furious flat-picking guitar style that has influenced generations of young pickers. Watson recorded a duet album with guitarist Chet Atkins, and was prominently featured on the Nitty Gritty Dirt Band's classic *Will the Circle Be Unbroken?*—an album that also included country legends Mother Maybelle Carter, Roy Acuff, Jimmy Martin, Merle Travis, and Earl Scruggs.

Jeannie C. Riley
IN HER BUS. WESTPORT. MASSACHUSETTS. 1973

Riley had a huge hit with her very first effort, "Harper Valley P.T.A.," a Tom T. Hall–penned tune about a young woman living with small-town hypocrisy. The song won the Country Music Award for Single of the Year in 1968. She also was one of the first female country singers to wear miniskirts and go-go boots. Riley's second effort was also top-ten—"The Girl Most Likely"—and she seemed to be on a roll. But soon the hits stopped coming and she renounced her past efforts, moving on to the field of Christian music, a career path many country singers take when their secular career heads south.

Hank Snow

GRAND OLE OPRY, NASHVILLE, TENNESSEE, 1974

One of the greatest country stars ever, the "Singing Ranger" had a huge career, which included almost fifty years (1936–1984) recording for the same record label, RCA Victor. Snow was born in Liverpool, Nova Scotia, and joined the Grand Ole Opry in 1950. His biggest hits came in the 1950s and 1960s: "I'm Moving On," "The Golden Rocket," and "The Rhumba Boogie." But perhaps his most notable contribution was as a salesman. He helped convince Elvis Presley's parents to allow their boy to sing secular music, allowing Snow's manager at the time, Colonel Tom Parker, to take on Elvis and "invent" rock-and-roll.

Holy Modal Rounders

AENGUS STUDIOS. FAYVILLE. MASSACHUSETTS. 1972

Pete Stampfel and Steve Weber are not your average country stars. Legendary characters in the Greenwich Village folk scene and the antiwar, pro-drug culture that followed, their music was purely traditional, in the style of old-time musicians and string bands of the 1920s and 1930s, such as Uncle Dave Macon, Gid Tanner and the Skillet Lickers, and Charlie Poole. In their original songs and lyrics to older tunes, they managed to slip in a number of psychedelic references. The Rounders made two influential albums in the 1960s on Prestige Records and contributed to the soundtrack of *Easy Rider.* But their lasting contribution is helping to bring traditional music to an urban, educated audience—including the founders of the influential Rounder record label, who named their company after the band.

Anita Carter

Anita was one of Mother Maybelle Carter's sweet singing daughters and was blessed with a beautiful soprano voice. She began her career as a child—traveling, singing, and playing bass with her mother and talented older sisters, Helen and June (later, wife of Johnny Cash), as Mother Maybelle and the Carter Sisters. In the 1950s, the band worked as an opening act for the up-and-coming Elvis Presley. Very few female singers of her day (1950s and 1960s) were able to manage a solo career. Most were part of a family band or acted as a featured singer with a band fronted by a man. Nevertheless, Anita did record and perform on her own and also as a duet partner of Hall of Famers Hank Snow and Waylon Jennings. She also performed and recorded as a folk singer.

Stringbean (page 106)
GRAND OLE OPRY. NASHVILLE. TENNESSEE. 1972

Called Stringbean for his long and lanky look, David Akeman was a comedian and banjo player in the old-time country tradition. He told corny jokes and "frailed" his instrument, strumming down on the strings and lifting them up—a style that predated modern bluegrass banjo. In fact, Earl Scruggs, who popularized "modern" bluegrass banjo, replaced Akeman as the banjo player with Bill Monroe in 1945. While not known as a recording artist, Stringbean was popular in live performance. He was widely admired for his role as a cast member of the *Hee Haw* television show and as a member of the Grand Ole Opry (1948–1973). Tragically, Stringbean and his wife, Estelle, were murdered during a robbery attempt in their home.

Archie Campbell greeting a fan (page 107)
GRAND OLE OPRY. NASHVILLE. TENNESSEE. 1972

It's important for a country entertainer to stay close to his or her fans—and not "get above their raising." Here, Archie Campbell takes time out during his performance to greet an admirer. Campbell had a long career as a singer and entertainer, but he was best known as a comedian, working on the Grand Ole Opry and starring in (and writing for) television's *Hee Haw*. At a time when most country comedians dressed in goofy hillbilly garb, Campbell broke new ground by dressing in more normal clothes, often even business suits.

Wilma Lee and Stoney Cooper
AT HOME. NASHVILLE. TENNESSEE. 1974

One of the most successful of many husband-and-wife acts in country music, Wilma Lee and Stoney, with their Clinch Mountain Clan, played traditional music with a strong hint of old-time gospel and bluegrass. They came up through the "minor" leagues, playing radio stations in North Carolina, Arkansas, and West Virginia (the popular *Wheeling Jamboree* on WWVA radio), before landing a job on the Grand Ole Opry in 1957. While Wilma Lee and Stoney had a few hit records in the 1950s and early 1960s, they were mostly live entertainers, traveling widely to spread their music and to make their living. Wilma Lee remained active as a solo act for many years after Stoney's death in 1977, until suffering a stroke on stage in 2001.

DeFord Bailey
GRAND OLE OPRY, NASHVILLE, TENNESSEE, 1974

A member of the original Grand Ole Opry cast, the physically tiny Bailey was discovered in 1926 while operating an elevator. On the show, he soon became known as "The Harmonica Wizard," and was especially popular for his uncanny ability to simulate the sound of a train on that instrument. But his musical career was regrettably short-lived. After he was fired from the show in 1941, due to changing musical styles or racism (depending on who's telling the story), he all but retired from music and ran a shoeshine stand in Nashville until just before his death in 1982. This photograph was taken on an "Old Timers" night, backstage of the Ryman Auditorium.

Nathan Abshire

AT HOME, BASILE, LOUISIANA, 1977

Cajun music is a hybrid of many styles, including country, blues, French Canadian, and Spanish. Occasionally, Cajun influence reaches a broad country audience, such as the music of the Grand Ole Opry's Jimmy C. Newman or Hank Williams's recording "Jambalaya." Still, as a Cajun accordionist, Abshire lived on the fringes of country music, playing with local Louisiana bands, such as the noted Balfa Brothers, recording widely and playing folk festivals around the world. This picture was taken at Abshire's home next door to the Bearcat Lounge, where he often played.

Bill Monroe (page 114)

TAKE IT EASY RANCH, CALLAWAY, MARYLAND, 1973

Monroe (1911–1996) was one of the genuine legends of American music. In the 1930s, he took traditional country music to a totally new place, adding energy and style and creating what we now know as bluegrass music. Past band members went on to great success of their own: Lester Flatt, Earl Scruggs, Jimmy Martin, Del McCoury, and so many more. But his influence went beyond bluegrass music. Elvis Presley's first single on Sun Records in 1955 featured a blues number ("That's All Right Mama," by Arthur "Big Boy" Crudup) on one side and a bluegrass tune ("Blue Moon of Kentucky," by Bill Monroe) on the other—a blending of black and hillbilly music that became known as rock-and-roll.

Charlie Monroe (page 115)

TAKE IT EASY RANCH, CALLAWAY, MARYLAND, 1973

Elder brother to Bill, Charlie Monroe had a long career of his own. He started performing with brothers Birch and Bill in the 1930s, and then as a duo act with Bill, known as the Monroe Brothers. The two went separate ways in 1938—Bill to the Grand Ole Opry and stardom and Charlie to smaller venues with his band, the Kentucky Pardners. The Pardners included several musicians who went on to great success, including Lester Flatt, who left Charlie to work for brother Bill, and Ira Louvin, who later teamed with his brother Charlie as the Louvin Brothers. Charlie Monroe came out of retirement in the early 1970s to play bluegrass festivals, until his death in 1975.

Jimmy Martin with daughter Lisa and a friend

GETTYSBURG BLUEGRASS FESTIVAL, GETTYSBURG, PENNSYLVANIA, 1974

Known as the "King of Bluegrass," Jimmy Martin made his reputation early, when he played guitar and sang lead for some of Bill Monroe's greatest recordings (1949–1954). His distinctive voice, one of the most identifiable in bluegrass, has a strong hillbilly kick, leading to comparisons with that of the legendary George Jones. Since the mid-1950s he has been working with his own band, the Sunny Mountain Boys, a band that has turned out many future bluegrass stars, such as J. D. Crowe and Doyle Lawson. While Martin has had a few country hits—notably the classic truck-driving hymn "Widow Maker" and his signature "Sunny Side of the Mountain"—he has been primarily a touring act.

Del Reeves

GRAND OLE OPRY, NASHVILLE, TENNESSEE, 1974

Franklin Delano Reeves has had a long career in country music, beginning when he was a teenager in North Carolina in the 1940s. He moved to the Bakersfield, California, area—home of Buck Owens, Merle Haggard, and many other country greats—in the 1950s and made an aborted foray into rock-and-roll. Then moving to Nashville in the 1960s, he finally found a home. Many Del Reeves songs are novelty in nature and a lot of them mention girls and trucks. "Girl on the Billboard" was probably his biggest hit (1965). Then there was "The Belles of Southern Belle," "Women Do Funny Things to Me," "Looking at the World Through a Windshield," and "The Philadelphia Fillies."

Lester Flatt

GRAND OLE OPRY. NASHVILLE. TENNESSEE. 1972

Flatt and Earl Scruggs made up Flatt and Scruggs, the most commercially successful bluegrass band ever. They worked for Bill Monroe in the mid-1940s, raising the bar for all future bluegrass bands. Flatt contributed strong baritone vocals and guitar runs, while Scruggs popularized three-fingered banjo picking. Together, they toured widely from 1948 until they disbanded in 1969, playing for traditional country audiences and for younger, college-educated audiences, such as at the Newport Folk Festival. They even recorded a live album at Carnegie Hall. Their hits included 1962's "The Ballad of Jed Clampett," the theme for television's *Beverly Hillbillies* and "Foggy Mountain Breakdown," the theme for the 1967 film *Bonnie and Clyde*.

Emmy Lou Harris

AT HOME, LOS ANGELES, CALIFORNIA, 1980

Surviving the folk/rock/country bands of the early 1970s, Emmy Lou has had a highly successful and influential career. She first came to prominence for her work with the legendary Gram Parsons, who blended country music and rock in the Byrds and the Flying Burrito Brothers. On her own, she has led several bands over the years, with an emphasis on traditional music. Part of her success comes from the quality of her collaborations. Her past band members include Vince Gill, Ricky Skaggs, and Rodney Crowell, and she had hits as a trio with Linda Ronstadt and Dolly Parton. Still, her biggest assets are her beautiful voice, tasteful material, and simple grace on stage.

Kitty Wells (page 124)

LONE STAR RANCH. REEDS FERRY. NEW HAMPSHIRE. 1981

Born Muriel Deason, Kitty Wells was one of the first great female country singers, a huge influence on Patsy Cline, Loretta Lynn, and others who followed. With a dignified performing style and a strong honky tonk voice, she and husband Johnny Wright comprised one of country music's most enduring acts—over sixty years in the business. Kitty's breakthrough came in 1954 when she answered Hank Thompson's megahit "Wild Side of Life" with her classic "It Wasn't God Who Made Honky Tonk Angels," which pinned the blame on men, not God, for causing "many a good girl to go wrong."

Johnny Wright (page 125)

LONE STAR RANCH. REEDS FERRY. NEW HAMPSHIRE. 1981

Johnny Wright was a cabinetmaker and a banjo player and fiddler when he met and married eighteen-year-old Kitty Wells on October 30, 1937. Johnny also teamed with Jack Anglin from 1938 to 1963 and the two, as Johnny and Jack, produced many fine recordings combining bluegrass with a hint of honky tonk. They backed Kitty on "It Wasn't God Who Made Honky Tonk Angels" and had several hits of their own, including the often-covered "Poison Love" in 1951 and the no. 1 best-seller "(Oh Baby Mine) I Get So Lonely" in 1954. After Anglin's death in 1963, in a car wreck on the way to Patsy Cline's funeral, Johnny had a no. 1 hit on his own in 1965, the patriotic "Hello Vietnam."

John Duffey

TAKE IT EASY RANCH. CALLAWAY. MARYLAND. 1973

Duffey was the mandolin player and high tenor for two of the most influential newgrass bands ever: the Country Gentleman and Seldom Scene. Loosely defined, "newgrass" refers to the generation of bluegrass musicians who came after Bill Monroe, adding a more contemporary attitude to the music, while still following and respecting the Monroe style. Duffey helped formed the Country Gentlemen in 1957 and the Seldom Scene in 1971, remaining with that band until his death in 1996. The latter band, named for the fact that they rarely toured, was one of the most popular bands in bluegrass in the 1970s and into the 1980s, often performing with more mainstream acts such as Linda Ronstadt.

Roy Acuff

GRAND OLE OPRY. NASHVILLE. TENNESSEE. 1973

Roy Acuff lorded over the Grand Ole Opry from 1937 virtually until his death in 1992. More of a live act than a recording star, Acuff's most creative period came early with signature hits "Great Speckled Bird" and "Wabash Cannonball" in the late 1930s through the late 1940s. Though he was a crooning singer, his band's sound was purely "old-time," and featured ace Dobro picker "Bashful" Brother Oswald. Acuff wasn't your average hillbilly singer. His dad was a lawyer, not a farmer or factory hand. And he had political aspirations of his own, running for governor of Tennessee twice (as a Republican). Most of all, Acuff was an astute businessperson, cofounding Acuff-Rose in 1942, arguably the most important music publisher in the industry, featuring the priceless Hank Williams catalog.

Jimmy Dickens (page 130)

INDIAN RANCH. WEBSTER. MASSACHUSETTS. 1974

Jimmy Dickens was one of the preeminent country entertainers of the 1950s and 1960s. A typical Dickens show featured rhinestone suits, corny country jokes, fine ballad singing, and signature novelty songs, such as "May the Bird of Paradise Fly Up Your Nose," his no. 1 hit song of 1965, "Take an Old Cold Tater (and Wait)," and "Out Behind the Barn." His diminutive size—he is under five feet tall—lent him the nicknames "Jimmy the Kid," "Little Jimmy," as well as ample opportunity to get laughs at his own expense. It also has provided him with hit songs such as "I'm Little, but I'm Loud." Dickens became a member of the Grand Ole Opry in 1948 and was inducted into the Country Music Hall of Fame in 1982.

Mac Wiseman (page 131)

INDIAN RANCH. WEBSTER. MASSACHUSETTS. 1972

Wiseman is one of those rare country musicians with classical music training, but it was his distinctive tenor voice and his ability to straddle the fence between country and bluegrass music that made his career. In 1946 he landed a job with Molly O'Day, one of the first female country stars, then sang and played briefly with Flatt and Scruggs and Bill Monroe before setting out on his own in 1950. Touring widely, Wiseman also worked as a record executive and had some hit records, notably "Jimmy Brown, the Newsboy" and "'Tis Sweet to Be Remembered." In the early 1970s, he reunited with Lester Flatt to make three records on RCA and became a perennial headliner at bluegrass festivals.

Joe Val

INDIAN RANCH. WEBSTER. MASSACHUSETTS. 1972

Val was a typewriter repairman in Watertown, Massachusetts, by day, but at night and on weekends he played mandolin and sang bluegrass in his acrobatic high-tenor voice. He worked at the Hillbilly Ranch with the Lilly Brothers and at Harvard with the Charles River Valley Boys, with whom he recorded the groundbreaking *Beatle Country* album in 1966— Beatles' music bluegrass style. Val later put together his New England Bluegrass Boys but died of cancer in 1985 at age fifty-nine just as his career started taking off nationally. Pictured on the left playing with Joe is fellow New Englander Jim Rooney, who later moved to Nashville and produced albums by Nancy Griffith, Iris Dement, and others.

Roscoe Holcomb

CAMBRIDGE, MASSACHUSETTS, 1972

Holcomb (1911–1981) played banjo, guitar, and harmonica and sang unaccompanied in a haunting piercing voice, which musician and photographer John Cohen dubbed the "high lonesome sound." Holcomb's roots were pre-commercial. He made his music in churches and dances, but made his living in the coal mines and in construction. Discovered and recorded late in life by Cohen, he toured briefly outside his home of Hazard, Kentucky, representing a rapidly disappearing musical style and way of life to a totally different audience, including Eric Clapton, who is said to have called Holcomb his favorite country musician.

The Country World of Henry Horenstein

Today country dominates American popular music. Country radio stations outnumber all others, and country music outsells everything but rock-and-roll. Indeed, Nashville, the music's national headquarters, has become the modern-day Tin Pan Alley, with its state-of-the-art production facilities, abundance of entertainment conglomerates, and sheer number of artists and cultural workers. Generating $1.5 billion in record sales alone, country music is indeed big business.

More than 2,100 radio stations feature country music today. Virtually all ignore older musicians, hits, and styles with a fervor that amounts to a blacklisting of all but the newest artists and the music manufactured to corporate specifications. A contemporary country music event is as likely to be an arena show as a roadside dance. Today's great country stars play the same stadiums, arts centers, and casinos as their pop and rock peers. An elaborate country tour will utilize dozens of vans and semitrucks, along with numerous technicians, roadies, and support staff. At these shows, devoted fans are no closer to their idols than they are at a Britney Spears, Dave Matthews, or Kid Rock event.

Henry Horenstein's photographs portray the world that preceded today's sophisticated country scene. Horenstein photographed local clubs, dance halls, and outdoor venues that hosted the music. In these images, Horenstein frames the run-down nobility of the Ryman Auditorium, once home to the Grand Ole Opry, the casual atmosphere of Tootsies Orchid Lounge, the community roots of Cajun dances. These images, and the hundreds more from this body of his work, form a remarkable archive of country music in transition in the 1970s. Portraits of artists, shots of workers and fans, and glances at the places where country music lived all transport us to a world so close in time, yet so distant in spirit.

Hillbilly Fever

The country music world of thirty years ago did not resemble this modern system of mass-marketed entertainment and mainstream acceptance. The most important country stars have always won national fame and coast-to-coast exposure on radio, records, and the stage. Yet until recently, the broader world of country music—the bedrock of lesser-known artists, business people, and fans—was largely set off from the mainstream of American entertainment. As Henry Horenstein rightly points out, country music thrived everywhere in the United States. Yet the music flourished in a series of largely unheralded local and regional scenes, sustained by tight-knit communities and cemented by intense loyalties and personal relationships.

After World War II, country music flourished throughout America. War workers and servicemen brought their tastes for rural sounds with them as they migrated for defense jobs or military duties. These migrants created and strengthened thriving country music markets in cities such as Baltimore,

TOP:
Lester Flatt and Bill Monroe,
Backstage at the Grand Ole Opry,
Nashville, Tennessee, 1972

BELOW:
Jerry Clower,
Grand Ole Opry,
Nashville, Tennessee, 1973

Chicago, Cincinnati, Los Angeles, Boston, and Washington, D.C. The relatively new technologies of the electric pickup and magnetic tape transformed modern recording and country music. New genres—bluegrass and honky tonk country—grew from the collision of rural and urban cultures. Thousands of taverns filled with half-a-million jukeboxes became centers of working-class entertainment. There country music entered a golden age that lasted for three decades, an era evoked by famous names that still define the music for so many: Hank Williams, Ernest Tubb, Flatt and Scruggs, Patsy Cline, Lefty Frizzell, Ray Price, Kitty Wells, the Maddox Brothers and Rose, Moon Mullican. The music thrived in roadside inns and dance halls, its pronounced beat inviting all but the shyest or clumsiest onto the floor. Songs of love and loss, of soul-searching pain and stoic acceptance jostled with anthems of hard living and good times. Keening steel guitars, mournful fiddles, cutting guitars, and propulsive banjos all made country a significant stream of American popular music.

Boston Boy

Henry Horenstein's life embraces the golden age of this honky tonk music, its fading and renaissance. Born after the war, he was a young boy during the high times of electric hillbilly music and the founding generation of bluegrass. He came of age as a member of a younger generation whose appreciation for country both gratified and inspired older musicians. Horenstein grew up listening to country, but it was as a young adult and novice photographer that he really immersed himself in traditional country and bluegrass music. While some rock-and-rollers began to borrow from and trade with country musicians in the 1960s and 1970s, many in the rock-and-roll community came simply to love the music as it was. Profound cultural gaps between older traditional fans and younger listeners were bridged or ignored by a common love of the music. As the folk revival in the 1950s and early 1960s had seen educated and middle-class listeners lovingly embrace mountain and blues music, ten years later many of the counter-culture would find country and bluegrass music that spoke to them. Horenstein was part of that generation, even as he loved country from his childhood.

The roots of country music lay in Southern hills and rural life, but country music has always had a stronghold in American cities. Boston and its surrounding area was no exception. The city and suburbs have long nurtured a thriving country music community: local Boston radio featured live Saturday-night jamborees well into the 1950s, and country music package shows frequently stopped in the area. Disc jockeys Lynn Joiner and the late Brian Sinclair (both of "Hillbilly at Harvard") and Ed the Detective have featured old-time country on Boston radio for decades. The Boston area also had thriving folk and bluegrass societies that have, for decades, brought to town pioneering artists for concerts, dances, and workshops. Horenstein grew up in this environment, where country music was present on the airwaves and in clubs and roadhouses.

Historically minded, Horenstein entered his studies at a fortuitous time. The exciting and crucial redirection of history in the 1950s and 1960s saw scholars emphasizing the importance of everyday experience. For these writers, such as E. P. Thompson and Herbert Gutman, common people in any society were the unsung and crucial makers of their history. Perhaps most significant, Horenstein learned the historical importance of class, the attention to the economic and social relations of those at different social levels. For country was the music of working people, and Horenstein's photos repeatedly and eloquently show us the working-class roots and branches of country music. Whether in the images of the care-worn and simply dressed patrons of the Hillbilly Ranch, the hard-living denizens of Tootsies Orchid Lounge, or those anxiously and expectantly lined up outside the Grand Ole Opry, Horenstein's photos show us that country music is firmly rooted in the everyday lives of American working-class people.

Y'All Come

These images show a now largely vanished world of country-music parks and outdoor venues that regularly hosted the best in honky tonk and bluegrass. New River Ranch, Sunset Park, Watermelon Park, Sleepy Hollow Ranch, and many others all featured national artists and local favorites. Here, families regularly congregated on weekends, making all-day excursions to play outdoors, picnic, listen to their favorite music, and mingle with their idols. Even the greatest stars of the Grand Ole Opry regularly toured these parks and roadhouses, in between Opry package tours and weekly appearances at the Ryman Auditorium. Country music royalty such as Bill Monroe, Roy Acuff, Johnny Cash, Mother Maybelle and the Carter Sisters, and Kitty Wells, the queen of country music, all played these parks regularly, as did local acts. And of course all these shows featured more than the stars. The great sidemen, the pickers, and backup musicians all had their turns in the spotlight: Buck Graves, the great Dobro man, playing flashy solo turns with Flatt and Scruggs; electric guitar pioneer Billy Byrd, stepping up for take-off leads with Ernest Tubb; fiddler Mack Magaha sawing on the strings with Reno and Smiley.

These photos beautifully capture the local working-class worlds of country music and the close community of artists and fans. Fans and stars ate together; smoked and joked; swapped photos, recipes, and stories, before and after show time. Stars performed their latest hits, answered requests, for obscure B-sides, and hawked souvenirs and songbooks. Afterward, they signed autographs and posed for pictures for hours, before climbing into cars and buses to make the next gig further up the road. The fans hung on every note, every phrase, every corny joke and routine. They admired the latest spangly suits and dresses on their favorites, colorful outfits made by Nudie the Rodeo Tailor and Nathan Turk of Hollywood. Sometimes they even pitched in to wash or repair an item between sets. Children played in the woods and on makeshift playgrounds. Those starstruck kids with talent and heart were glued to the front of the stage, drinking in every note and every turn of phrase. Many a country career began when an encouraging headliner invited a young five-year-old on stage to sing a Hank Williams classic. And the next week would see a different bill, a different star, and a whole new round of pickin' all day and "dinner on the ground."

Hillbilly Heaven

Like any successful artist, Horenstein was a child of both talent and luck; his pictures are not only arresting but important, as he managed to capture historically significant images. Horenstein frequented the Opry in its last years at the Ryman Auditorium in downtown Nashville before it was

TOP:
Vassar Clements,
Holiday Inn,
Cambridge, Massachusetts, 1973

BELOW:
Jethro Burns,
Renfro Valley Jamboree,
Renfro Valley, Kentucky, 1976

Hazel Dickens,
Arnold Arboretum,
Boston, Massachusetts, 1978

moved permanently out to the Opryland amusement park. Here he caught historic images—Bill Monroe and Lester Flatt, long estranged but recently reconciled. Horenstein captured DeFord Bailey, an Opry star of the 1930s and the first African-American country celebrity. He secured the image on one of Bailey's only return visits to the Opry. Horenstein not only sought the great stars but also the supporting players, photographing little-known Opry pioneers like Fiddlin' Sid Harkreader as well as longtime stars Hank Snow and Archie Campbell. We see Louis Marshall "Grandpa" Jones on the Opry stage, now grown into the role he created as a young man in the 1930s. We then see Grandpa's old friend Stringbean backstage at the Opry, framed between a young girl and his own publicity still. By giving us the unheralded as well as the famous, Horenstein remains true to a historical vision that puts the common and everyday ahead of celebrity and commerce. In these images, E.P. Thompson meets Hank Thompson.

Horenstein's eye captures details and clues. In his photograph of Ernest Tubb surrounded by adoring fans, we can see the pen with which he would sign autographs for hours after each performance. Background vocalist Carol Lee Cooper stands at the mirror right before show time, her book of lyrics and chord changes right at hand. Her parents, Wilma Lee and Stoney Cooper, pose in their den, framed by an earlier portrait, done in the early 1950s; overlooking the scene are photos of the publishers Fred and Wesley Rose, who played important roles in their careers. Connie Smith wears a striking cross, revealing that she had already dedicated herself to religion while still performing secular music. Such portraits all present musicians on their own terms: Neither flattering nor harsh, Horenstein's camera offers visions of country musicians and their fans as people who occupy different sides of the stage but who have everything else in common.

Phases and Stages

By the late 1960s, country music venues were attracting another audience along with working people and their families. Young adults, usually city-bred and middle-class, came in search of the music. Spurred on by the folk revival, younger "citybillies," as they were sometimes known, came to hear a music far from their roots but close to their hearts. Many of these newer fans were hippies, whose long hair and unconventional dress may have raised some eyebrows but whose enthusiasm and sincerity generally earned them a warm welcome.

Horenstein's camera shows us that by the 1970s, this country music world, so long self-sufficient, had fallen inexorably under outside influences. From rock-and-roll came a loosening of the country dress codes; iconoclastic artists such as Waylon Jennings in these photographs look as much like hard rockers as country legends. While rock-and-roll offered one alternative for country style, the synthetics revolution brought about another. Horenstein shows traditionalists like Stonewall Jackson, Connie Smith, and Jean Shephard adopting contemporary polyester leisure suits and dresses, even as peers Porter Wagoner and Johnny Wright remained loyal to the Nudie rhinestone look. The light weight and easy care of the polyesters (compared with the heavy yet fragile rhinestone ensembles) made these styles much more attractive to many artists. Bill Monroe dazzles in a vertigo-inducing jacket, while Kitty Wells evokes a rain forest in her stage gown. Longer hair and sideburns came to country as well, as artists claimed a look once primarily associated with truck drivers and rock-and-rollers. Conway Twitty's magnificent pompadour reminds us of his rockabilly days when, as Harold Jenkins, he tore up roadhouses from Newport, Arkansas, to Ontario.

But more than just the look of country was changing. The eclipse of this music and these venues says much about the social changes and cultural workings of American life in the past forty years. The parks, roadhouses, and bars in Henry's photos coexisted in a fragile yet stable ecology. Artists, promoters, club owners, and fans all participated in a system in which one hit record could sustain a career for years through loyalty, hard work, and a modest profit motive. Not only did artists and fans enjoy long-term relationships, but promoters, club owners, and venue operators also worked for many years with artists, agents, and one another. Promoters booked the same acts for decades, working their children into the business. (Two generations of the Waltman family ran Sunset Park in Pennsylvania for more than sixty years!) But ultimately, the whole economy began to change. The major record labels began a long cycle of consolidation and contraction in the early 1970s. They eventually purged their rosters of steady but unspectacular sellers. The overwhelming multimillion record sales in the 1970s of the *Saturday Night Fever* soundtrack compelled labels to devote excess energy to seeking blockbuster hits while channeling fewer resources to so-called marginal markets such as country.

By the mid-1980s, when Horenstein took a break from photographing musicians, few of his subjects still had major label record deals, or indeed any deal at all. While independent record companies like Rounder and Rebel signed bluegrass artists such as the Johnson Mountain Boys or J. D. Crowe and the New South, they could not always provide a home for Opry stars like Jean Shephard. Without new records to promote and sell, artists had fewer revenue sources. The centralization of entertainment in corporate hands further undermined this country music scene. Taverns closed, and entertainment shifted to the confines of home. National promotion, cable television, and corporate theme parks all crowded out small-scale operators.

Busted

Most important, the face and place of the audience was changing. The inexorable contraction of family farming and the transfer of that land to development and corporate interests (what we might call "rural renewal") destroyed many jobs that sustained the country audience. Long recessions in the Ford and Reagan eras saw deindustrialization and job loss. Fewer workers were making or buying those Torinos and Bonnevilles we see in these photos. Population shifts in the Northeast and Midwest found workers heading for different jobs and for lives in the South and Southwest. Post-1965 immigration to the United States created a new working class with vastly different traditions and tastes. In short, the changes that remade American life after 1970 put an end to the fragile country music world Horenstein chronicled in these photos.

While young people from all walks of life and musical backgrounds filled the ranks of traditional country fans in the 1970s, there was no denying the aging of the audience and of the artists. Corporate

Jean Shephard, backstage,
Grand Ole Opry,
Nashville, Tennessee, 1972

TOP:
Osborne Brothers,
Bobby and Sonny,
Gettysburg Bluegrass Festival,
Gettysburg, Pennsylvania, 1974

BELOW:
John Cohen (left), of the New Lost
City Ramblers, with Don Reno,
of Reno and Smiley,
University of Chicago Folk Festival,
Chicago, Illinois, 1969

marketers have long favored youth and ignored older consumers; as long as that pattern held true, country would not be a growth industry locally or nationally. When country music did receive a major commercial boost in the late 1980s, it came from a singer who adapted the arena techniques of rock-and-roll shows and who sold himself with marketing strategies he studied in college: Garth Brooks. Suddenly, country found a much larger and younger audience. Good-bye Hillbilly Ranch, hello MCI Center.

A Way to Survive

Most of the venues, and many of the performers seen in Horenstein's photographs, are no longer with us. But although the country music parks have faded, and the Hillbilly Ranch is gone, the music that filled them all lives on, tenuously but tenaciously. If country radio ignores its roots, you can find them throughout the nation on public radio and the Internet. The commercial margins of American music are more sizable today than they were in the past. Many who make, hear, and preserve traditional sounds neither seek nor desire overarching mainstream success. They pursue their calling with an eye on the same modest profits that once sustained the old economy. As long as such ventures can break even and grow sufficiently, music matters more than market share.

Older musicians, styles, and songs persist, rediscovered, remade, and preserved by a coalition of younger artists, new audiences, and longtime fans. Dolly Parton, Johnny Cash, and Merle Haggard today enjoy revived recording careers on independent labels. We are witnessing another in a series of resurgences in traditional country music, sounds strongly rooted in the folk musics of the Appalachians, Southwest, and West. The unanticipated and overwhelming success of the film *O Brother, Where Art Thou?* and its multimillion-selling soundtrack, has revealed a widespread hunger for older country sounds, sensibilities, and songs. That hunger is echoed in the continued respect and reverence held by young people today for older country musicians such as Johnny Cash, Willie Nelson, George Jones, and Ralph Stanley.

We can welcome the publication of these unseen photographs as part of this moment of preservation, reconsideration, and renewal. Henry's images always turn us back to the music. They direct us to traditional country, whether we locate it in a slick new CD box set or a battered 78 unearthed at a Salvation Army store. Anita Carter's beatific photo invites us to listen to her aching country classic "Is This My Destiny?" Jimmy Dickens's portrait reminds us that he was a consummate balladeer as well as an entertainer. Horenstein's shot of Jerry Lee Lewis captures all his swagger as well as his vulnerability, and we recollect that he had a long career as a country hitmaker after his rocking years.

Henry Horenstein has made a career of loving, quirky, and honest engagement with small subcultures hidden from the mainstream. These music photos offer a vision of enduring art in a slowly changing world. His work thus takes its place in the larger process of preservation and memory that is central to country music's history, and indeed central to American culture.

—**Charles F. McGovern**
National Museum of American History
Smithsonian Institution

Photographer's Notes

While I do not photograph musicians exclusively, I have done quite a bit of it over the years. Sometimes it has been for professional reasons—for promotional purposes, album art, magazine stories, and so forth. But usually the work has been personal—done for myself and anyone who cares to view it. I take the pictures and hope to find a home for them later. It can take a while. In fact, most of the pictures in *Honky Tonk* were taken more than twenty-five years ago, and few have been published previously.

The reasons I photograph music as a subject are twofold: I like music, and I think it's an important part of our culture and should be recorded visually, as well as on audio. I suppose I'm killing the proverbial two birds with one shot—by playing and working at the same time.

Most of the photographs in *Honky Tonk* were made with equipment and techniques that are long outdated. I would never recommend them to an aspiring photographer today. But for the record, this is what I used. The square-format pictures were made with a Rolleiflex Wide 2¼-x-2¼-inch twin-lens reflex medium-format camera—a wonderfully designed instrument and fairly obscure. Only about four thousand were made between 1961 and 1964. I owned two of them in the 1970s and used them whenever possible to achieve negatives that were dead sharp and rich in detail.

When I took photographs outdoors with the Rolleiflex, I usually used natural light. Indoors, and when there was low light outdoors, I used a very simple portable bare bulb flash—an electronic flash bulb without a reflector—to brighten the room with relatively soft, diffuse light. Whenever possible, I used a tripod, outdoors and in, to ensure accurate framing and no camera movement while I exposed the film.

The rectangular pictures were made with various Leica M-series 35mm rangefinder cameras—usually M-2 or M-4 models—with 28mm and 35mm wide-angle Leitz lenses. Many photographers are familiar with this classic combination. I used Leicas to achieve sharp, rich negatives and also for their small size, convenience, and unobtrusiveness. I used flash—again a bare bulb—if I had to, but I always used natural light, if there was enough, even if it meant pushing film development to compensate when the light was too low.

I almost always used Kodak Tri-X film, whether for medium-format or 35mm shots. This is a general-purpose film that still works remarkably well twenty-five years later—assuming you want black-and-white photographs. I shot the photos for *Honky Tonk* in black-and-white because it didn't occur to me to shoot in color. Back then, black-and-white materials were considered far more "artistic" than color, which was yet to come into its own aesthetically and technically. Given my druthers, I still use black-and-white film today. But this is an individual choice. I just like the way black-and-white photographs look; they seem more timeless. Also, they are more permanent—less likely to fade with time—and this fits with my general goal of using the camera to record "history."

Henry Horenstein,
photographing backstage,
Renfro Valley Jamboree,
Renfro Valley, Kentucky, 1976
© Bob Hower

Photographing musicians these days can be difficult. There is more awareness of the value—promotional and monetary—of a photograph than there was when I was taking these pictures in the 1970s. Today, many musicians won't let you photograph them unless they have approval rights over what's to be used. They may also try to restrict your rights so you can't use the photograph to produce "product," such as posters, that might compete with their own merchandise.

I am hardly an objective source, but I think this attitude is very shortsighted. It leads to fewer photographs and ultimately less exposure for the musicians while they are actively working and even afterward. The freelance photographer provides an important service, which the musician doesn't have to pay for. This seems like a fair trade to me.

Acknowledgments

So many people helped out with *Honky Tonk*, over a very long period of time. I hope I remember to mention them all.

Certainly I should begin with Eddie Stubbs and Charlie McGovern for their wonderful written contributions, as well as their support, enthusiasm, and first-hand knowledge of country music and the times when these pictures were taken.

The late Brian Sinclair (a.k.a. Ol' Sinc), longtime disc jockey on WHRB's "Hillbilly at Harvard," added his considerable intelligence and humor to the book. May he rest peacefully in Hillbilly Heaven.

Fact checking was a challenge, since I made few if any notes when I took these pictures. I relied heavily on the good graces of Eddie, Charlie, and Sinc, as well as Ken Irwin and Bill Nowlin of Rounder Records, with additional support from Jeff Place and Cousin' Lynn Joiner. All are off the hook for any remaining mistakes, which are surely slips of my memory or research talents.

Emily Villemaire and George Bouret, master printers both, made final prints for the book. Jacquie Strasburger Dow cleaned up the prints spotlessly. Nashville's best photographer and good friend Lawson Little added his two cents, sharp eye, and fine companionship. Shannon Perich, at the Smithsonian Institution National Museum of American History, has been a great support and sharp editor of the photographs. Ditto for Sarah Morthland of the Sarah Morthland Gallery.

Putting any book together is a challenge and for this one I have the team at Chronicle Books to thank for connecting immediately with the pictures. They totally "got" it. Anne Bunn's enthusiasm and understanding of the subject was crucial in selling the original idea to her colleagues. Alan Rapp seamlessly picked up the pieces when Anne left for Boston, and I am grateful to him for his patience and his continuing commitment to the book. Brett MacFadden added a terrific and sensitive design and a sympathetic ear. Beth Steiner has done her best to get the final product look as good as it has. Thanks also to Leslie Davisson, Jan Hughes, Doug Ogan, Mimi Kusch, Azi Rad, and Laura Lovett—who supported and crafted the book from the very beginning to the end.

Janet Bush was an enormous help along the way in shaping *Honky Tonk*—in both content and look. Tom Gearty also helped over a period of time with many aspects of the book. Lawson Little, Lewis Rosenberg, and Robert Hower let me use their photographs of me, from way back when.

Additional thanks to Anne Tucker, Keith Carter, Robert Rindler, Jim Dow, Lorie Novak, Byron Hollinshead, Lan Degeneres, Ingrid Krauss, Paul Langmuir, Cindy Charron, Jessica Coffin, Jen Kodis, Sandra Law, and Michelle Kloehn. Also, to Jim Smith and Rob Clifford of Clifford-Smith Gallery; John Cleary of the John Cleary Gallery; Kira Florita, Carolyn Tate, Diana Johnson, and Denny Adcock of the Country Music Hall of Fame; and Gordy Brown of the New England Country Music Historical Society. To Christiane Robinson, for too much to tell. I am most grateful to all the musicians, singers, and fans who allowed me to record their lives, however briefly.

Ed Emberley's Complete FunPrint Drawing Book

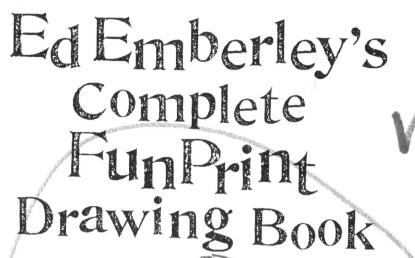

Little, Brown and Company

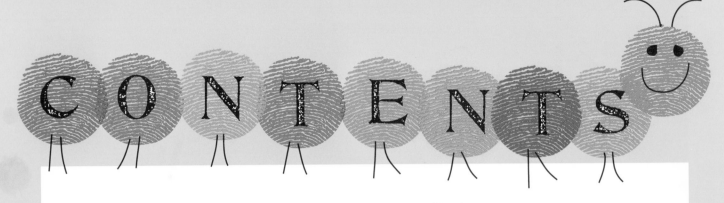

CONTENTS

Easy! Fun!

You can make FunPrints using
your fingers or your thumbs.
Use just the tip
to make small prints.

1. Press your
finger on an
ink pad

   or paint it
   with watercolor
   and a brush.

2. Press it on
your paper.

3. Let it dry.

4. Draw.

FOR INSTANCE

PERSON

(JUST A LINE CAN MAKE A HAT.)

WALKING

FISH

BIRD

5

SPIDER

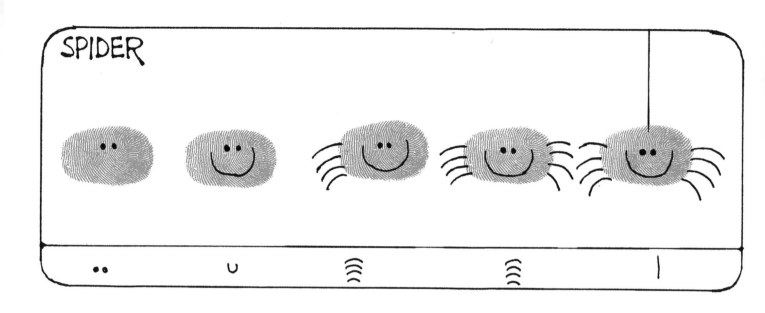

RABBIT

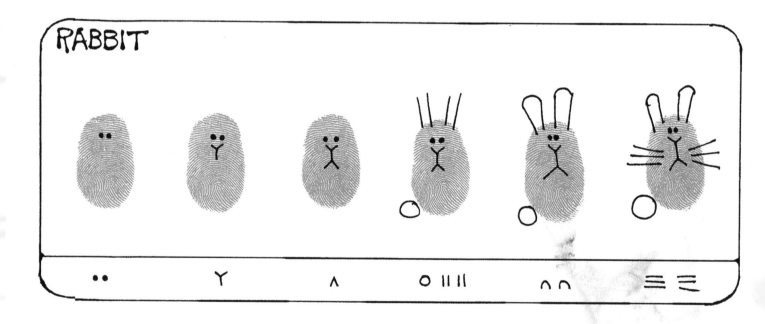

6

HALLOWEEN

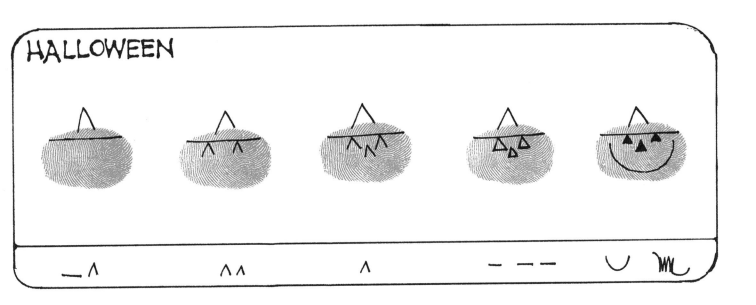

FROG

7

FOLKS

HAPPY

NOT HAPPY

LAUGHING

ANGRY

SLY

WORRIED

SHY

SPEAKING

WINKING

8

SHOUTING

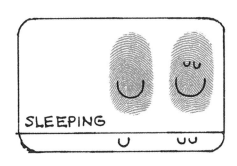

SLEEPING

WHISTLING

SCARED

SINGING

SMILING

CRYING

OTHERS

9

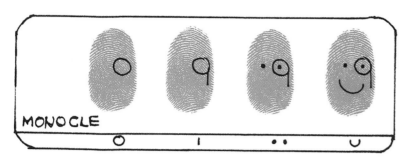

MONOCLE

○   I   ..   ∪

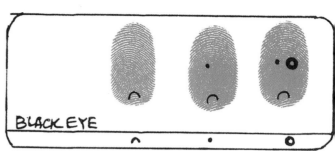

BLACK EYE

∧   .   ◉

GLASSES

○○   — — —   ..   ∪   LOOKING AROUND   SUNGLASSES

PIRATE

═   ∪   ₥   .   ∪   >   ＼   ⁖⁘

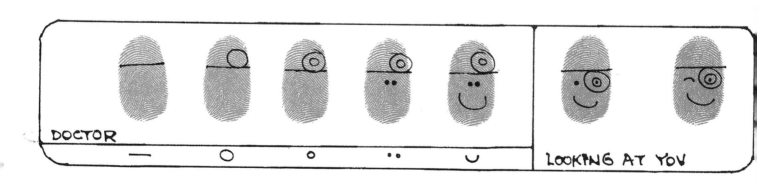

DOCTOR

—   ○   ○   ..   ∪   LOOKING AT YOU

10

CROOK

OTHERS

HAIR

SCRIBBLES MAKE GOOD HAIR, WHISKERS, SKIRTS AND SHAGGY DOGS.

HERE ARE SOME MORE SCRIBBLES AND SOME SPECKS AND SCRATCHES.

CAP — ∧ ○

HATS = ≋ = ≋

COWBOY = ( ) COWGIRL

FOOTBALL —)( )(|| SIDE VIEW

FIREMAN — ( ) (0

SKI CAPS — — ○ ETC.

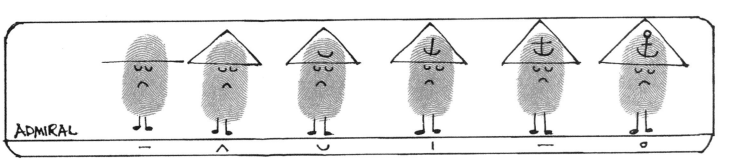

ADMIRAL

SAILOR

TURBAN

BAND PERSON

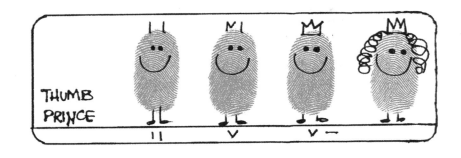

THUMB PRINCE

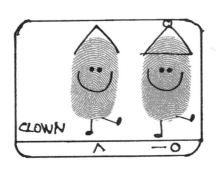

CLOWN

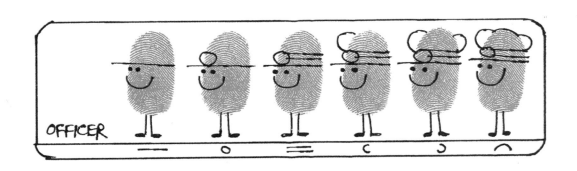

OFFICER

WALKING

WALKING
OVER
THAT WAY→

BACK VIEW

←

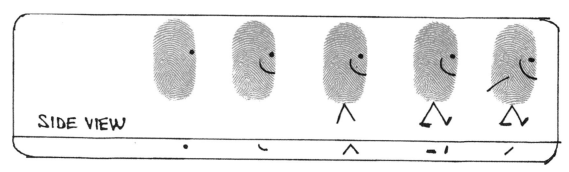

SIDE VIEW

RUNNING

KICKING

JUMPING

KNEELING

15

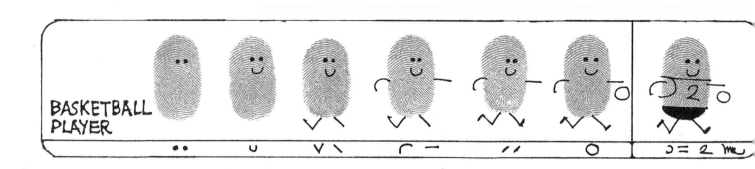

BASKETBALL PLAYER

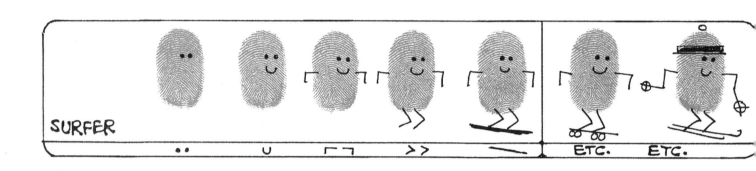

SURFER

BOXING

ETC.

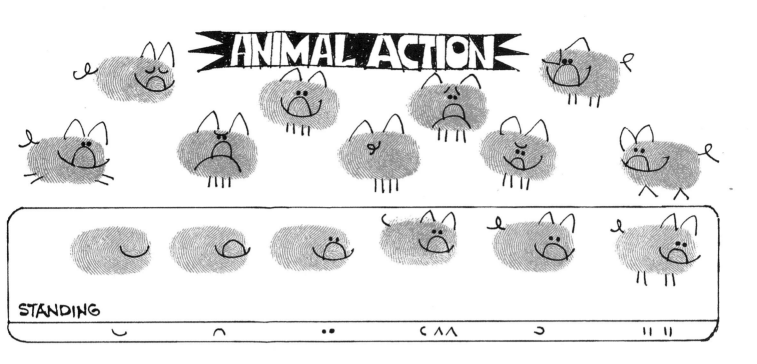

ANIMAL ACTION

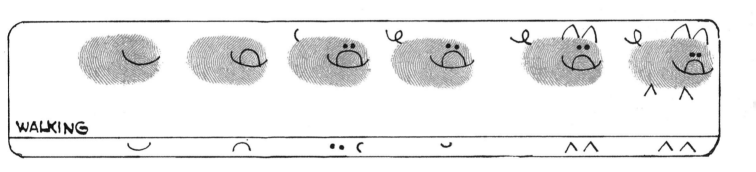

STANDING

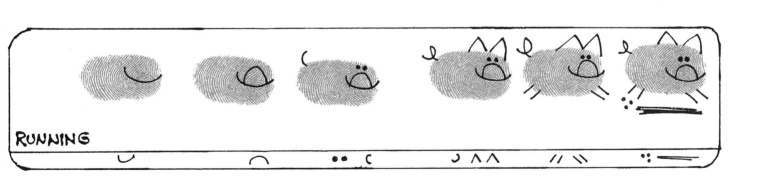

WALKING

RUNNING

SLEEPING

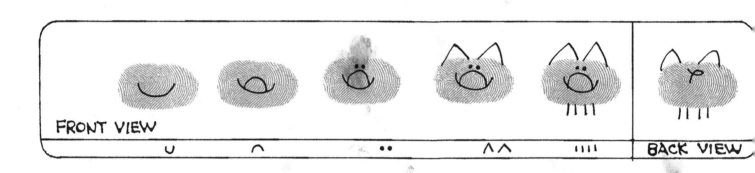

FRONT VIEW   BACK VIEW

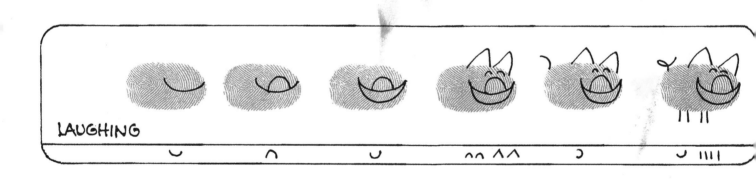

LAUGHING

WORRIED   ANGRY   SITTING DOWN   SINGING   PIGLET   JUMPING OVER

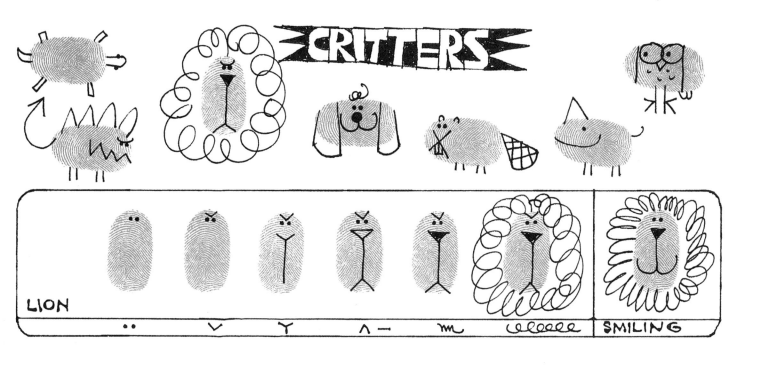

CRITTERS

LION

..   V   Y   ∧ —   m   eeeeee   SMILING

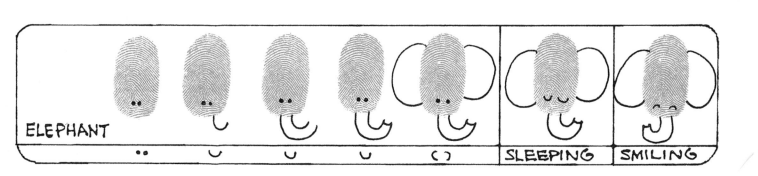

CAT

..   V   u u   — ∧∧   U uu uu   ≡ ≡   WINKING

ELEPHANT

..   u   u   u   ( )   SLEEPING   SMILING

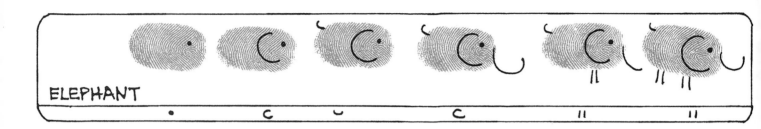

ELEPHANT

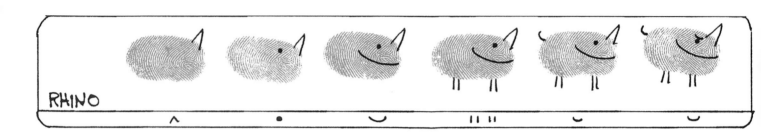

RHINO

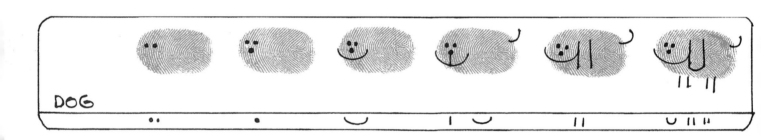

DOG

MONSTER

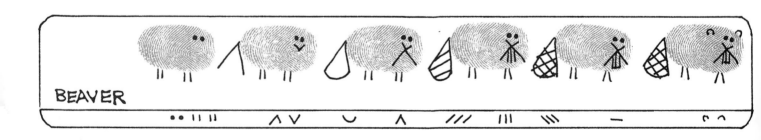

BEAVER

OWL

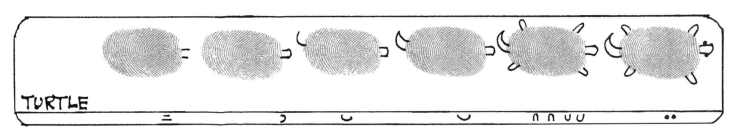

TURTLE

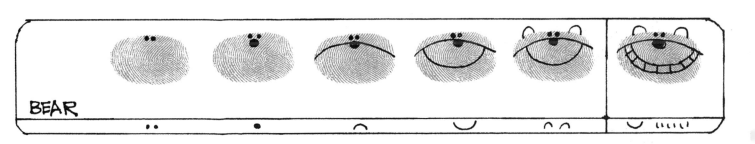

BEAR

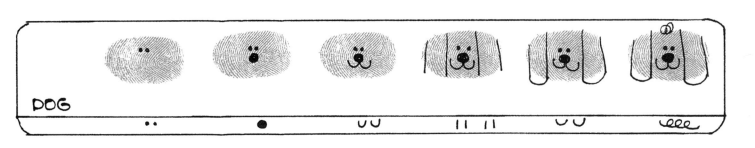

DOG

HAMSTER

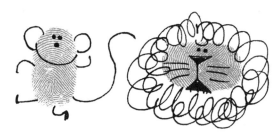

HAMSTER TOP VIEW

21

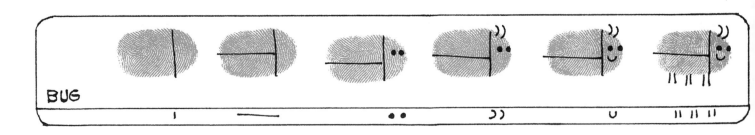

BUG

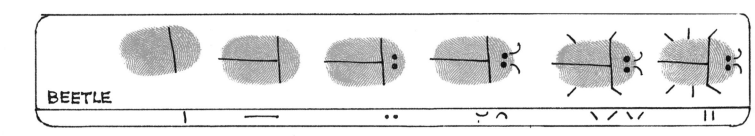

BEE

BEETLE

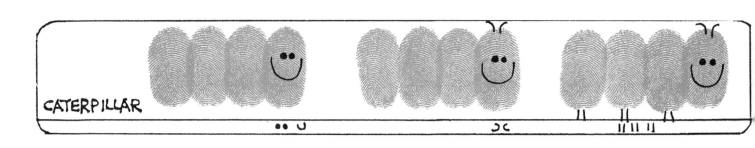

CATERPILLAR

BIRDS

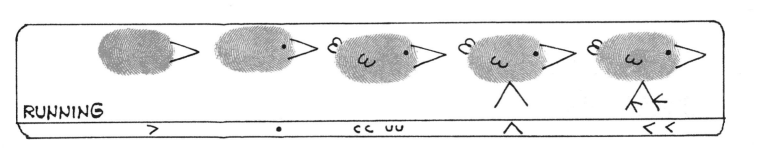

STANDING

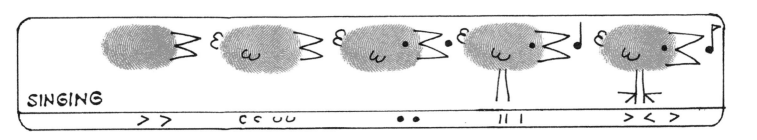

RUNNING

SINGING

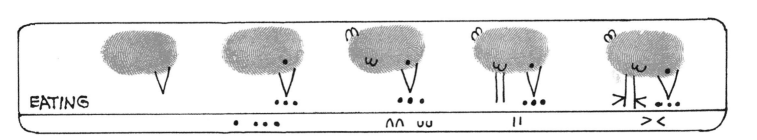

EATING

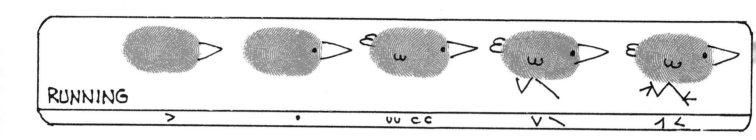

RUNNING

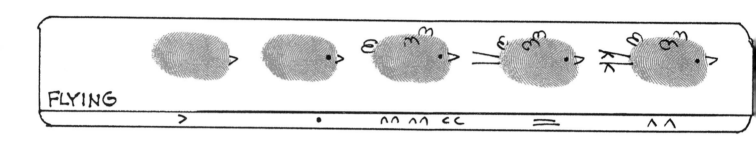

FLYING

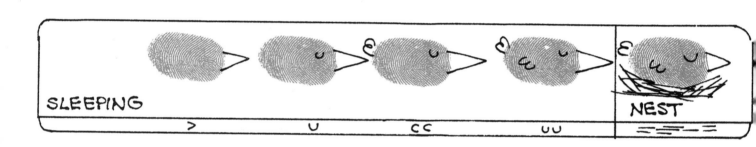

SLEEPING

NEST

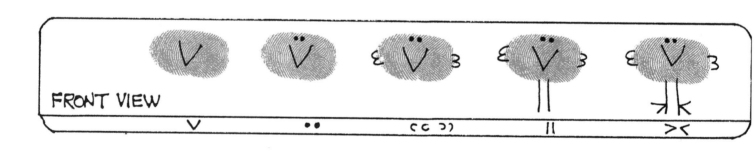

FRONT VIEW

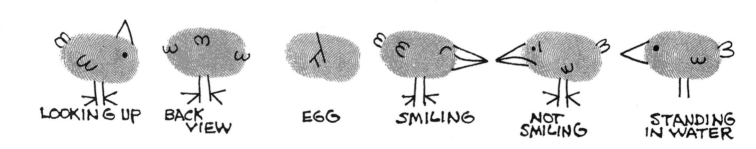

LOOKING UP   BACK VIEW   EGG   SMILING   NOT SMILING   STANDING IN WATER

HOLIDAYS

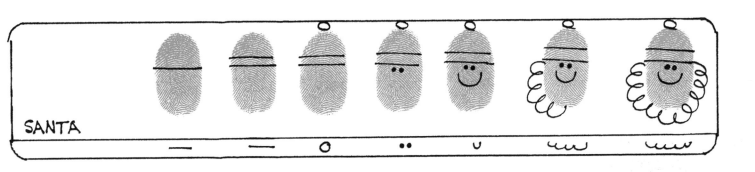

SANTA

FIRECRACKER

BIRTHDAY CAKE

UNCLE SAM

LINCOLN

HALLOWEEN

HALLOWEEN

GEORGE
WASHINGTHUMB

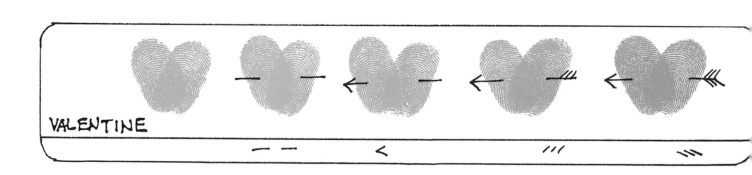

VALENTINE

26

PILGRIM

PILGRIM

EASTER
BUNNY

FLOWERS

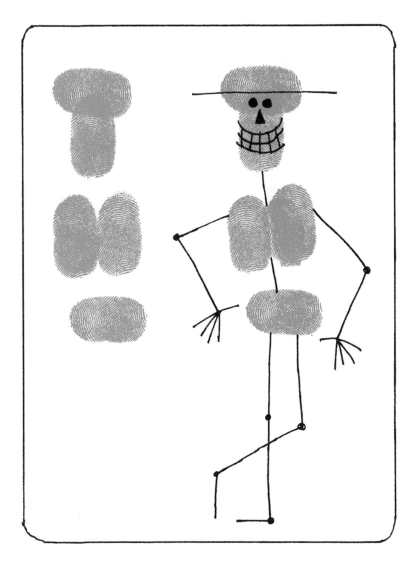

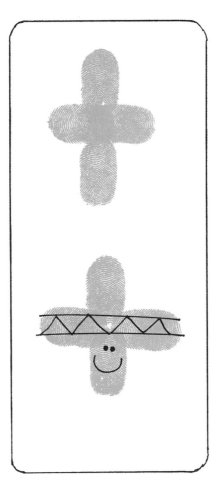

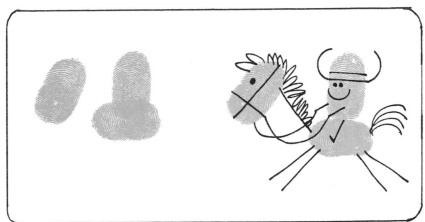

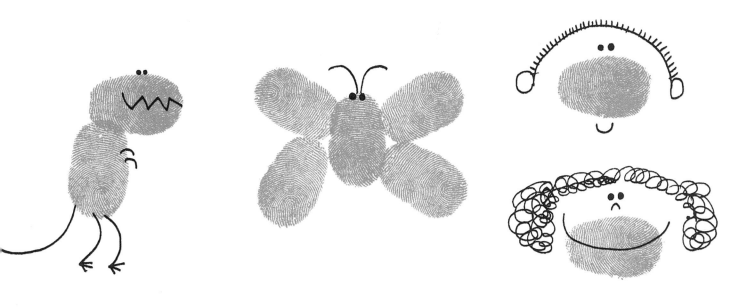

THE GARDEN

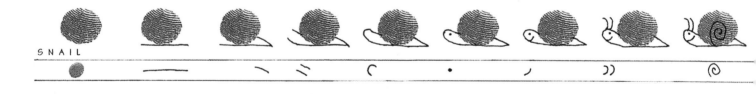

FLOWER

SNAIL

FROG

SMALL FLOWER

CROCUS

TULIP

BROWN ANT

CATERPILLAR

CENTIPEDE

BUMBLEBEE

THE POND

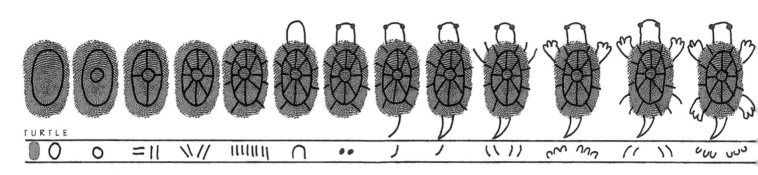

TURTLE

DUCK

POLLYWOG

BUTTERFLY

SWIMMING FROG

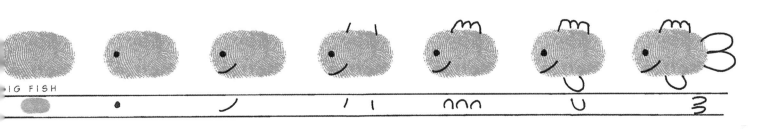

IG FISH

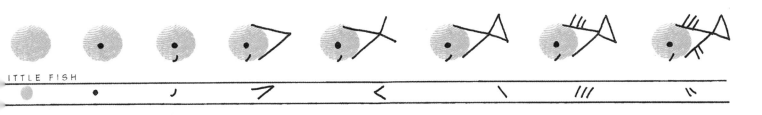

ITTLE FISH

37

FINGERLINGS

I ALSO CALL THESE MY
TEENY TINIES. I USE A
DIFFERENT FINGERTIP FOR
EACH COLOR.

SPRING

SUMMER

RABBIT

MOUSE

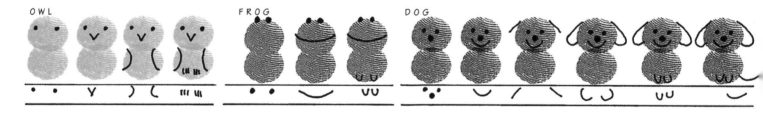

OWL

FROG

DOG

BEAVER

38

FALL

FALL

WINTER

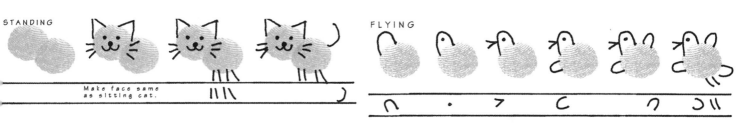

SITTING CAT

BIRD

STANDING

Make face same
as sitting cat.

FLYING

RUNNING

Make face same
as sitting cat.

PECKING

ANIMALS

ELEPHANT

BABY ELEPHANT

LION

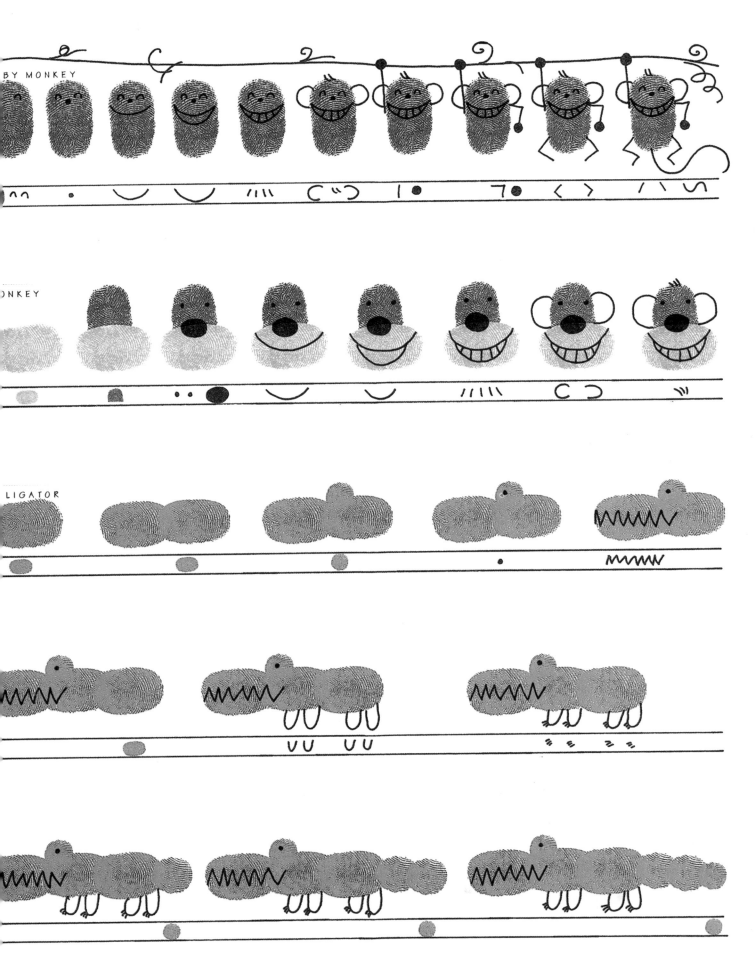

BY MONKEY

MONKEY

LIGATOR

MORE ANIMALS

RACCOON

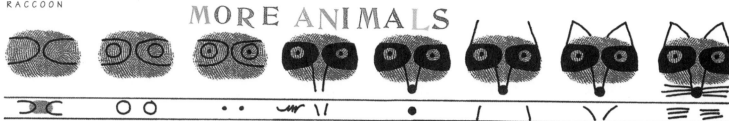

PIG

BEAVER

DOG

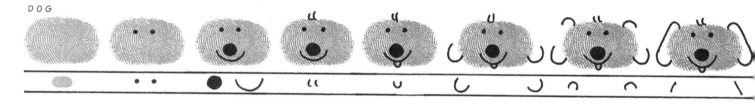

CAT

SMALL BULLDOG

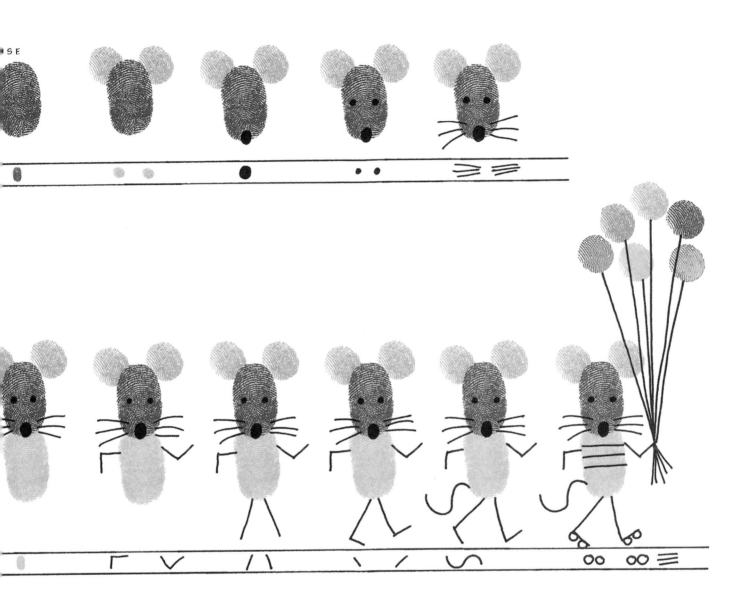

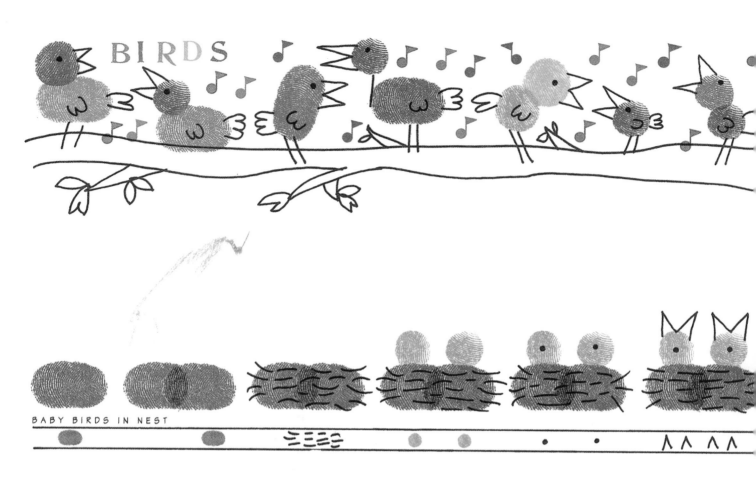

BIRDS

BABY BIRDS IN NEST

BIRD EATING WORM

BIRD FRONT VIEW

BIRD BACK VIEW

RD FLYING

RD SINGING

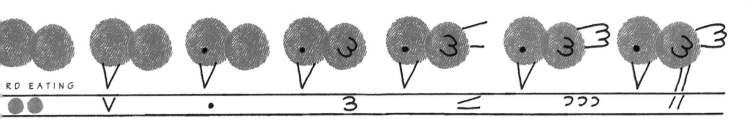

RD EATING

RD WALKING

45

BEAN BUDDIES

I THINK FINGERPRINTS LOOK LIKE LITTLE BEANS. I LIKE TO USE THESE LITTLE "FINGER BEANS" TO MAKE ALL DIFFERENT KINDS OF LITTLE BEAN BUDDIES.

BASIC

PEA BEAN BUDDY   BAKED BEAN BUDDY   LIMA BEAN BUDDY   JELLY BEAN BUDDY

SPEAKING

HI!

POINTING

LOOK

YAWNING

HO HUM

CELEBRATING

HOORA

GRUMBLING

HRUMPH

WONDERING

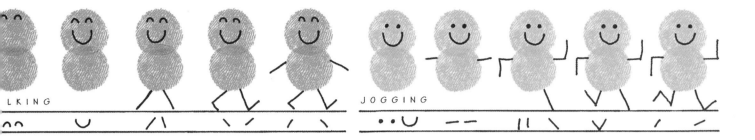

LKING

JOGGING

NNING

WINNING

LLET

HULA

OG
NCING

TAP DANCING

47

LITTLE CLOWN

NAPOLEON

SAILOR

QUEEN

KING

PRINCE

48

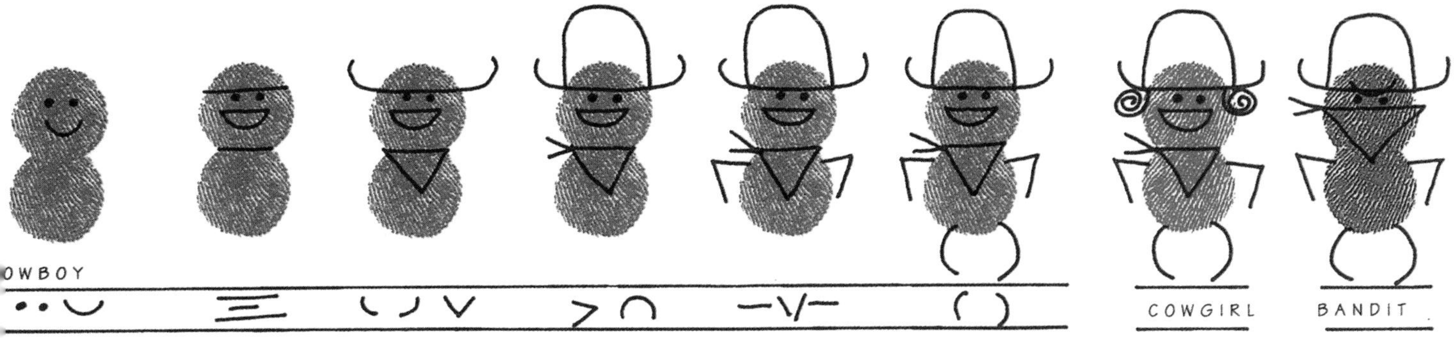
OWBOY
COWGIRL
BANDIT

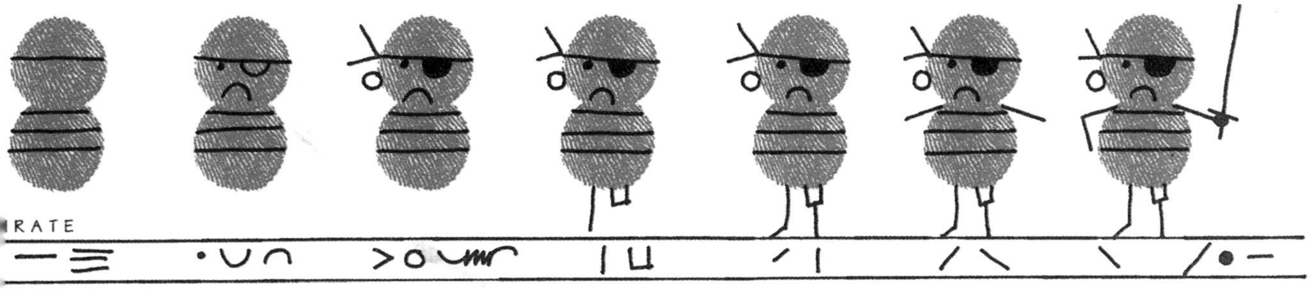
IRATE

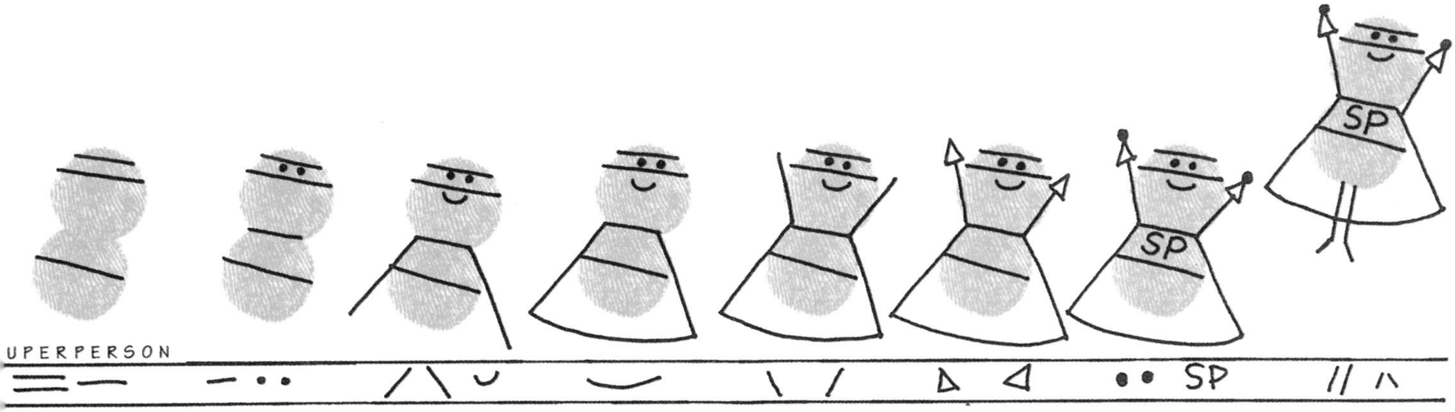
UPERPERSON
SP

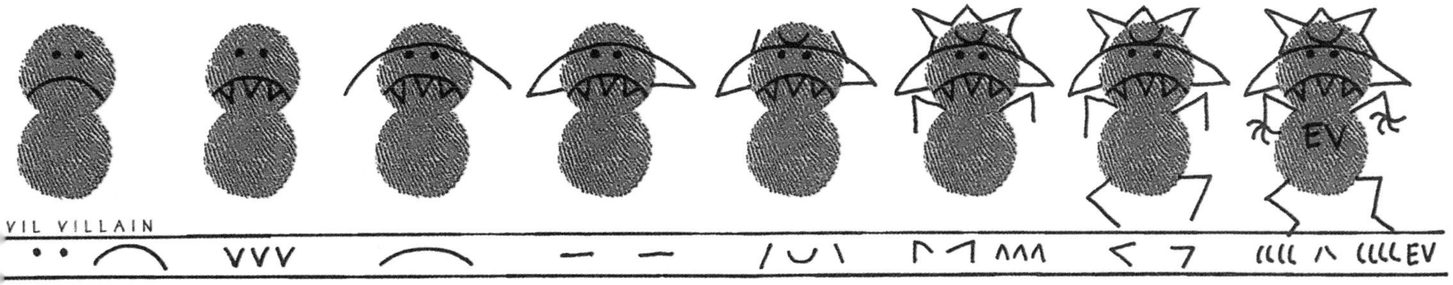
VIL VILLAIN
EV

FEELINGS

HAPPY

VERY HAPPY

VERY VERY HAPPY

SNOOTY

SAD

VERY SAD

VERY VERY SAD

UPSET

ANGRY

VERY ANGRY

VERY VERY ANGRY

SLY (MISCHIEVOUS)

SHY (EMBARRASSED)

SUSPICIOUS

HURTING

MUSIC

HUMMING

WHISTLING

SINGING

SINGERS

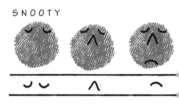
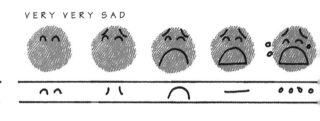
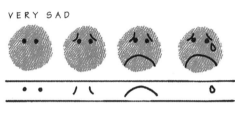
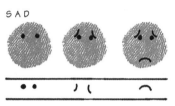

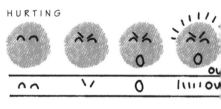

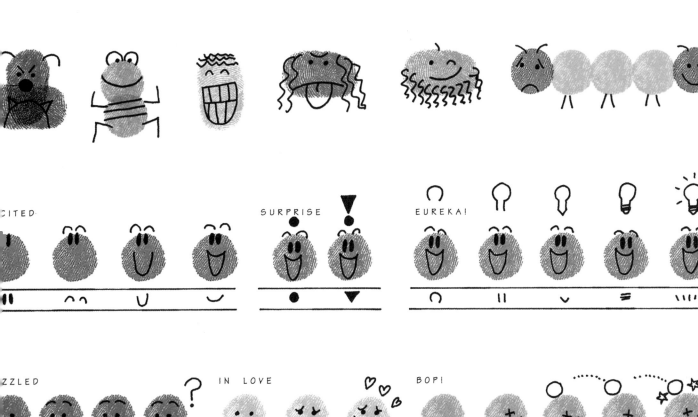

SURPRISE

EUREKA!

CITED

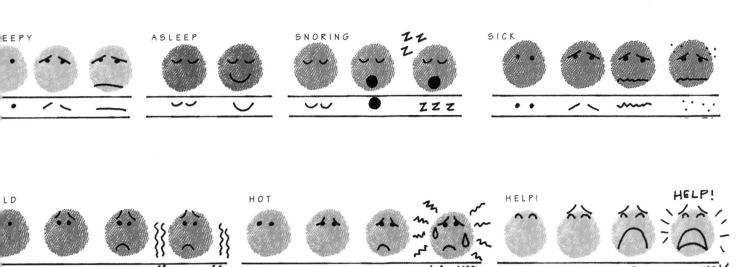

ZZLED

IN LOVE

BOP!

EEPY

ASLEEP

SNORING

SICK

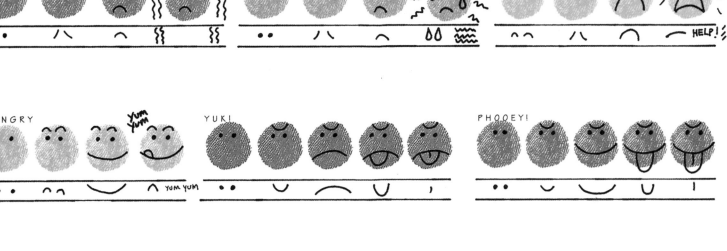

LD

HOT

HELP!

NGRY

YUM YUM

YUK!

PHOOEY!

SPRING FUN

SKIPPING ROPE

BICYCLING

SKATEBOARDING

ROLLER-SKATING

IL SHOWERS

HING

KING

TES

SUMMER FUN

CHASING BUTTERFLIES

SWIMMING

SURFING

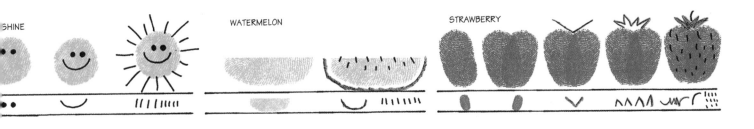

SHINE

WATERMELON

STRAWBERRY

WN
WING

NBATHING

ASEBALL

FALL FUN

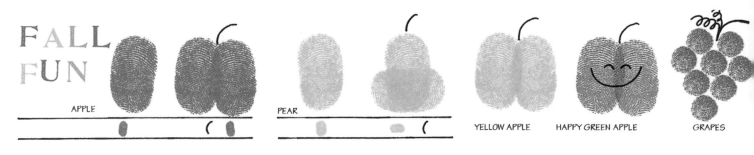

APPLE

PEAR

YELLOW APPLE HAPPY GREEN APPLE GRAPES

FARMING

LACROSSE

SOCCER

BALL

RTS FAN

CHEERLEADER

SKETBALL

WINTER FUN

PENGUIN FRONT VIEW

PENGUIN SIDE VIEW

SNOWPERSON

HOLIDAYS

EASTER BUNNY

EASTER EGG

CHOCOLATE EGG

CHICK

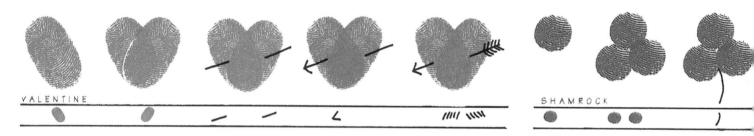

VALENTINE

SHAMROCK

LEPRECHAUN

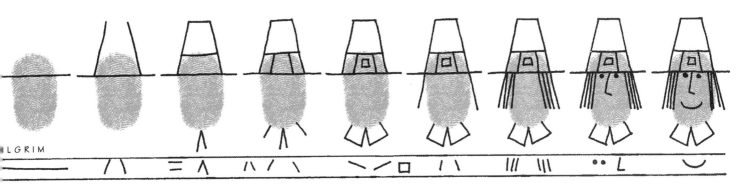

PILGRIM

TURKEY

PILGRIM

INDIAN

61

HALLOWEEN

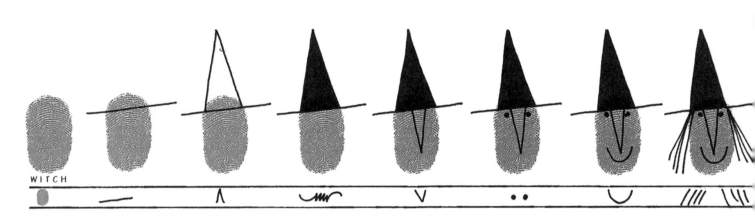

WITCH

FLYING WITCH

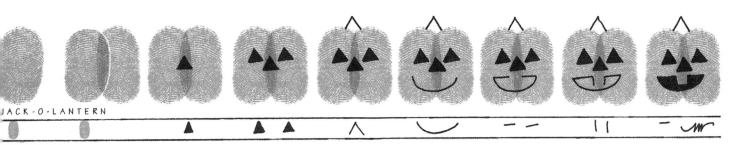

JACK-O-LANTERN

BAT

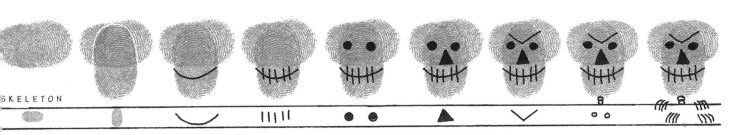

SKELETON

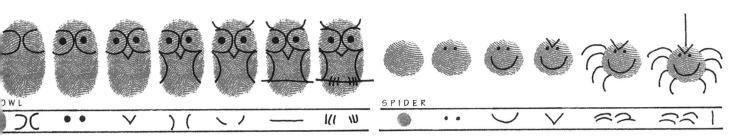

OWL

SPIDER

CAT

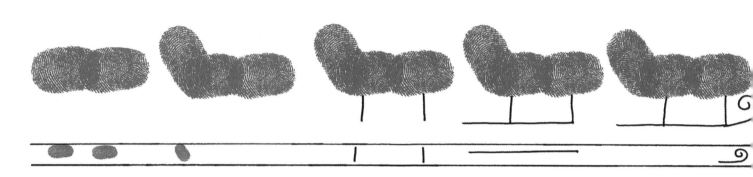

JINGLE   JINGLE   JINGLE

LAND SEA AND AIR

CAR

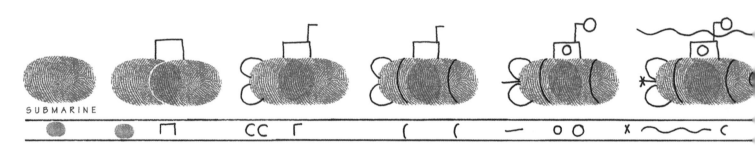

SUBMARINE

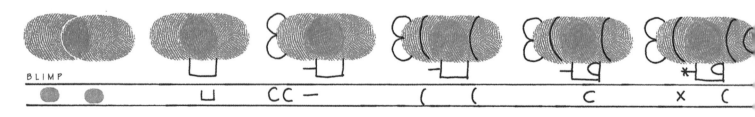

BLIMP

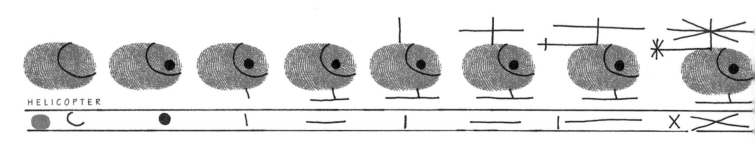

HELICOPTER

TRAIN

NGINE

OAL CAR

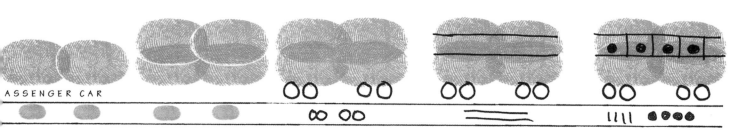

ASSENGER CAR

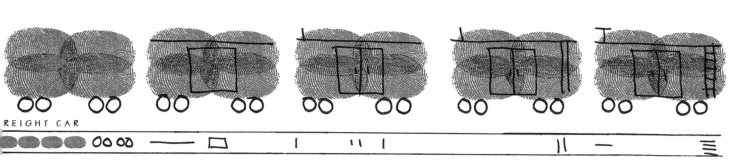

REIGHT CAR

RAINBOW CLOWN

COO COO

68

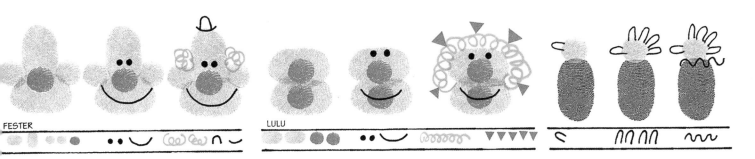

FESTER

LULU

RAINBOW DRAGON

LION

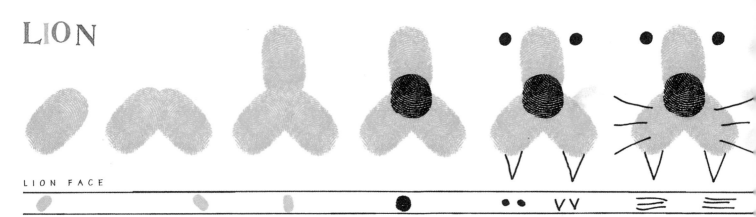

LION FACE

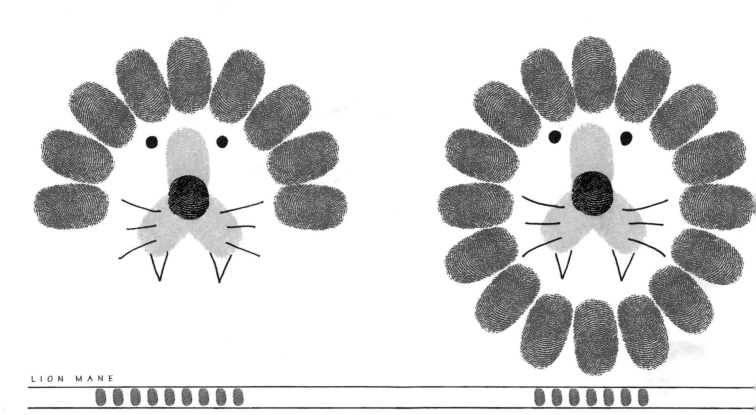

LION MANE

RAINBOW
LIONS

S K E T C H B O O K

HERE ARE SOME FINGERPRINT
THINGS I COULD NOT FIT INTO THIS
BOOK. CAN YOU FIGURE OUT HOW
I MADE THEM?

74

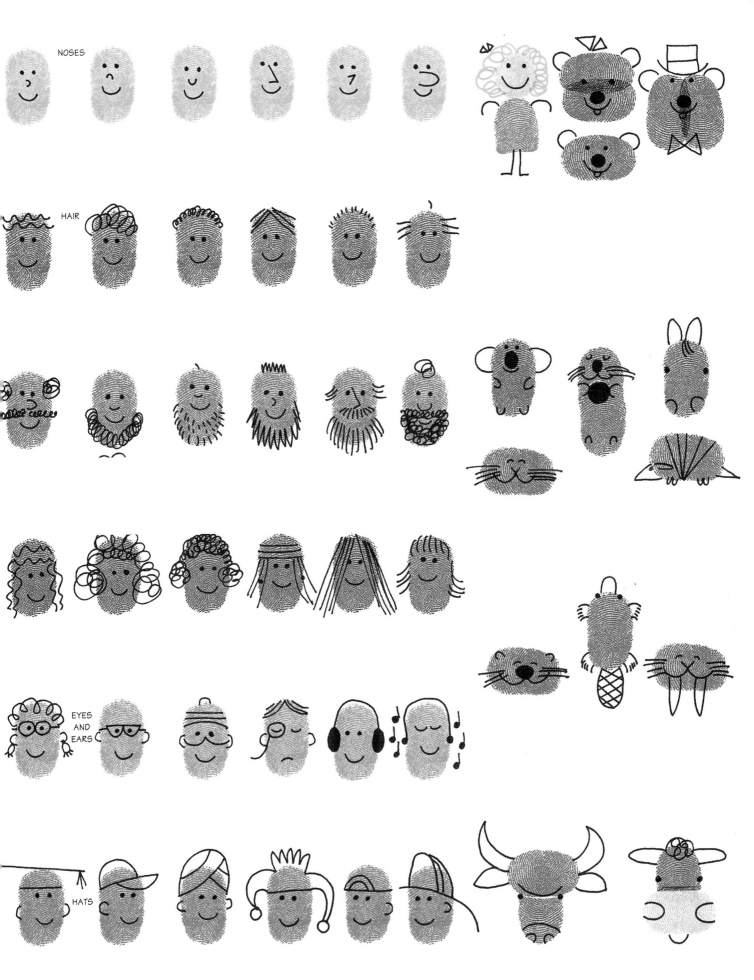

NOSES

HAIR

EYES
AND
EARS

HATS

ADVANCED FINGER-PRINTING

FOR THE ADVENTUROUS—
JUST A FEW OTHER WAYS TO COMBINE PRINTS,
COLORS, SIMPLE LINES, AND SOME
IMAGINATION TO MAKE PICTURES.
THERE ARE LOTS LEFT FOR YOU TO DISCOVER.
HAPPY DISCOVERING!

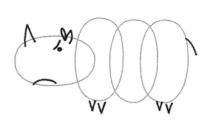

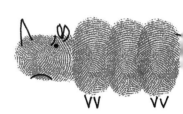

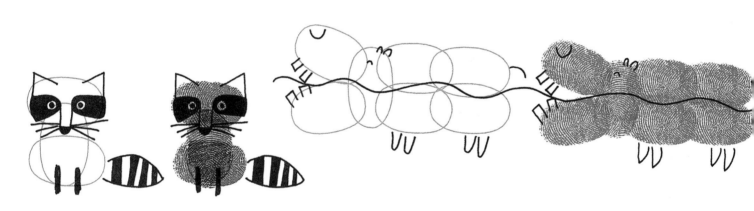

Something very special.

Just as no two fingerprints look just alike, no two fingerprint pictures will ever look just alike. Prints will be lighter or darker, lines will be thicker or thinner, colors will be different.

That means that no other fingerprint pictures will look just like the ones in this book, or just like yours. That's what will make your pictures "something very special."

VERY SPECIAL

More Ed Emberley Drawing Book Fun!

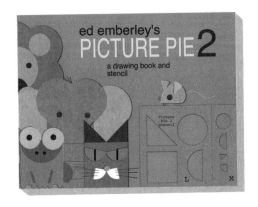

ED EMBERLEY'S DRAWING BOOK
OF ANIMALS

ED EMBERLEY'S DRAWING BOOK
OF FACES

ED EMBERLEY'S PICTURE PIE,
A CUT AND PASTE DRAWING BOOK

ED EMBERLEY'S PICTURE PIE TWO,
A DRAWING BOOK AND STENCIL

THE WING ON A FLEA:
A BOOK ABOUT SHAPES

ED EMBERLEY'S DRAWING BOOK,
MAKE A WORLD

ED EMBERLEY'S
BIG GREEN DRAWING BOOK
ED EMBERLEY'S
BIG ORANGE DRAWING BOOK
ED EMBERLEY'S
BIG PURPLE DRAWING BOOK
ED EMBERLEY'S BIG
RED DRAWING BOOK

DINOSAURS, A DRAWING BOOK
BY MICHAEL EMBERLEY

First Edition

From the previously published books by Ed Emberley
GREAT THUMBPRINT DRAWING BOOK (copyright © 1977)
and
THE FINGERPRINT DRAWING BOOK (copyright © 2000)

ISBN 0-316-73429-2

10 9 8 7 6 5 4 3 2 1

WOR

Printed in the United States of America